JUDO
The Gentle Way

Judo is the study of harmony, of circles, of controlled movements, beautifully conceived and executed with swiftness, precision and flair

JUDO
The Gentle Way

Alan Fromm *4th Dan*
and
Nicolas Soames *1st Dan*

Routledge & Kegan Paul
London, Boston and Henley

This book is dedicated to the Japanese Judo Masters Kenshiro Abe, 8th Dan, and the late Masutaro O-Tani, 8th Dan, in acknowledgment of their significant contribution to British Judo.

First published in 1982
by Routledge & Kegan Paul Ltd
39 Store Street, London WC1E 7DD,
9 Park Street, Boston, Mass. 02108, USA and
Broadway House, Newtown Road,
Henley-on-Thames, Oxon RG9 1EN
Set in 10 on 13pt Palatino by
Rowland Phototypesetting Ltd, Bury St Edmunds, Suffolk
and printed in Great Britain by
St Edmundsbury Press, Bury St Edmunds, Suffolk
Plates printed by
Headley Brothers Ltd, Ashford, Kent

Library of Congress Cataloging in Publication Data

Fromm, Alan, 1943–

Judo, the gentle way.
1. Judo.   I. Soames, Nicolas, 1950–
II. Title.
GV1114.F75   796.8'152   81-17850

ISBN 0-7100-9025-0   AACR2

Contents

Plates

Preface

It is in the nature of sport that the sportsman trains for specific competitions. Sport is often dominated by the concept of training in order to 'peak' at certain points and it doesn't seem to matter whether the status is amateur, professional or semi-professional. Where the ultimate goal is considered to be success in a competition then the attitude towards training is set in a fixed pattern, building up to the big day and relaxing afterwards – either in euphoria having won or in depression having lost.

However, there has recently been a move away from this pattern. Increasingly, people are enjoying a physical activity such as jogging, and even reaching quite high standards of fitness, stamina and technique, without the goal of the Fastest Marathon on Earth. Much the same trend is noticeable in the Judo world and it is to stimulate and encourage this, and to give pointers on training, that this book has been written.

In a sense, the very combat nature of Judo highlights the drama of competition; so easily can personalities clash because of the direct physical involvement of two people in a Randori or Shiai. We suggest, however, that only when competition is regarded as an aid to bringing out the best of ourselves, rather than a route to a medal, can the marvellous flavour of Judo be fully appreciated.

Conventional, competition-oriented Judo is limited in many ways. It is difficult really to enjoy hard, punishing training routines undertaken partly out of fear because of the big day looming ahead. If we are lucky, when the big day comes, we are on form and we win. If we are unlucky, we may have a slight cold or we might come up against an opponent who has made a speciality of countering our favourite attack, and we may lose. It seems that months of training have been wasted, our self-esteem hits an all-time low, and we may decide to take up ping-pong instead.

It happens also in the world of music that a pianist or a violinist will train furiously for a competition, win it, and then sink without trace, having been unable to cope with the aftermath because his vision was set only on that one day. The same applies to Judo. Success in a competition does not guarantee continued contentment within the Judo world subsequently.

The true artist, however, trains at his discipline because he regards it as a training for life. The Judoka who practises Judo as an art rather than as sport trains because he needs it, as he needs food to sustain, to stimulate, to satisfy him. Competition becomes a way of taking the temperature, so-to-speak; it highlights areas that may need attention, that may have fallen into disrepair. But it is only one aspect of Judo and certainly not more important than a daily training.

The difficulty is that so many of us have been conditioned to train with the competition in mind, and without that sense of urgency we become lax and even apathetic: we start to miss training sessions, and when we go to a Dojo, we talk too much or fail to put in as much effort as we really know we should.

In looking at the finer points of Judo, and drawing on the related practice of meditation, *Judo – The Gentle Way*, suggests that the ideal of a balanced human being and a highly skilled Judoka is a far greater aim than any medal and suggests ways of attaining it.

Not surprisingly, therefore, the emphasis is on developing the skills of Judo, not on knock-down contest techniques. It is certainly more difficult, initially, to work at mastering the skills of fast, light, precise Judo than the cruder Judo that results from heavy confrontation – but we believe it is, in the end, more satisfying. Ultimately, it is up to every individual Judoka to try different approaches with an open mind and then decide for himself.

Acknowledgments

We would like to thank many people for their help in the preparation of this book. Our greatest debt is to Nagabodhi of the Western Buddhist Order who wrote Chapter 6 and Danny Keene, 2nd Kyu, who exercised great skill and patience in the work on the drawings. The Yoga teacher, Michael Scherk, prepared the section on Yoga, selecting the Asanas of particular benefit to the Judoka (he is himself a 3rd Kyu) and he gave the matter much thought. Joan Graham, too, brought the experience of her Yoga practice to the simple, but highly effective Yoga drawings. We also thank Brian Ferrier for his action photographs taken in the Sobell Centre, London.

We owe a debt of gratitude to Trevor Leggett, 8th Dan, who, despite being very busy, gave us time and the benefit of his unmatched experience, as a Judoka who personally knew the major historical figures, and as a Judoka who is himself the distinguished author of a series of fine books on Judo. Others, too, including Marcus Kaye, 5th Dan, Charles Palmer, 8th Dan, and Philip Hammerton, 3rd Dan, were helpful in providing original material and/or checking the accuracy of the history chapter. Thanks also go to Sampson Sampson, 3rd Dan, Simon Mazullo, 3rd Dan and Chris Hobbs, 3rd Dan, for their skilled and patient work in the preparation of the illustrations, both drawings and some photographs. And Richard Bowen, 4th Dan, Vice-President of the Budokwai, who generously opened the photographic annals of the club.

1 The history of Judo

The development and expansion of Judo stands as one of the most extraordinary stories of the twentieth century. Few human activities have attracted more energy or thought than fighting in one form or another – in fact, formalized methods of combat are probably as old as mankind. Yet in the closing years of the nineteenth century there appeared a new collation of techniques which, while based on traditional, age-old principles, contained a number of innovations which made it into not just an effective form of self-defence when practised at the highest level, but an art form too.

The rapid growth of Judo which, within a few decades established a widespread and dedicated following, was a testament to its universal appeal. But why should Judo have any relevance in a twentieth-century world dominated by sophisticated weaponry systems far easier to acquire than such a difficult, elusive skill? Why should a very specific and almost rigid code of manners be accepted and even protected in a world growing increasingly informal in all its social dealings? And why should a difficult and alien language be retained as the language of the art? Ultimately, how is it that a world increasingly ruled by Western thought, Western aims and Western principles can be captivated by a practice that stemmed from one small country in the East which has itself become more Western than the West?

There is no one answer to these questions except the magic of Judo itself. Those who do not practise Judo will never understand it. Those who do cannot understand the bewilderment of the uninitiated. It is as simple and as paradoxical as that. But there are some more tangible answers to be found within the history of Judo.

Although Dr Jigoro Kano founded the Kodokan at the Eishoji Buddhist Temple in 1882, the beginnings of Judo are to be found in the Bushido tradition of the Japanese warrior class, the Samurai. Until the beginning of the Edo period (1603–1868), the highly trained Samurai practised their fighting arts primarily as a practical skill. Civil war was constant and although battle was often formalized with much proclaiming of rank and history before individual combat, the skills of the sword, spear, bow, staff, war fan and, of course, unarmed combat, had to work to be of any use. It is important to note, however, that the warrior spirit which pervaded Japanese life was inextricable from the techniques and the fighting arts themselves. War in one form or another had become such a way of life for so many centuries that fighting itself became a natural form of expression.

Therefore, the peaceful Edo period presented the ruling Shogunate with the difficult problem of harnessing and re-channelling the accumulated energy of generations of fighting. The answer was typically Japanese and typically pragmatic. The fighting arts had traditionally been regarded as no better or worse than any other art, be it flower-arranging, the tea ceremony or calligraphy. The result, probably, of Chinese influence generally and Zen Buddhist influence specifically, the arts were regarded as mediums of self-development in addition to their external expression.

With the necessity for a practical fighting skill no longer required to such an extent as when civil war raged, the Shogunate was able to emphasize the importance of the self-development aspect of the martial arts, not least because there were certain living masters who embodied this principle. Among them was the swordmaster Ittosai (1560–1653) who promoted the attitude that to overcome opponents without having to draw the sword illustrated the highest level of swordsmanship.

The fact that moral principles became as important as techniques meant that higher levels of safety in training were required, and increasingly during the seventeenth and eighteenth centuries, bamboo swords replaced blades and wooden swords. Thus Kenjutsu, the Art of the Sword, became transformed to Kendo, the Way of the Sword, and as the Edo period progressed and then gave way to the Meiji Restoration, other martial arts followed suit – Iai-Jutsu became Iai-Do, Kyu-Jutsu became Kyu-Do, Aiki-Jutsu became Aikido and Ju-Jitsu became Judo.

However much these transformations may have been part of a general trend, it always took the influence of individuals to effect a real change, and one of the most remarkable of these was Dr Jigoro Kano. The basic story is well known. Born in 1860 in the seaside town of Mikage, his family moved to Tokyo in 1871. A year later Kano began his study of Ju-Jitsu largely, he explained later, because he had poor health and an undeveloped physique and suffered from bullying. Ju-Jitsu at the time had degenerated considerably from the status it had once held. Training methods were often lax and even serious injuries were common – rarely were breakfalls formerly taught and those who continued training were very much the survivors. In short, Ju-Jitsu was widely regarded as the preserve of petty criminals. But from the start Kano was intrigued by the techniques. He trained at the Tenjin Shin-yo Ryu which specialized in Atemi-Waza or striking techniques and Katame-Waza or grappling techniques, and in 1881 at the Kito Ryu which specialized in Nage-Waza or throwing techniques. His continued persistence despite injuries demonstrated his keenness which extended also to a wide academic knowledge of the subject.

What is perhaps not so widely realized now is that Kano was extremely able academically and it was this combination of skill and culture which gave his Kodokan Judo the impetus not just to conquer Japan, but to penetrate worldwide.

By 1882 Kano was a skilled exponent of Ju-Jitsu and was ready, in the tradition of many outstanding martial arts figures, to form his own school. He was, however, very aware of the philosophical basis on which he wanted to build: his uncovering

3

of 'the principle of efficiency' was intended automatically to include moral as well as mechanical efficiency, in much the same way as it applied to other 'Do' forms.

Kano never claimed to discover anything new, but his synthesis of the variety of Ju-Jitsu techniques was sufficiently strong to have lasted intact with remarkably few changes to the present day. Of course, not only did he bring together the various aspects of throws, holds, strangles, chokes and armlocks, but he slightly modified where necessary to increase the safety factor, in the same way that the Shinai was introduced to Kendo. For example, Osoto-Gari was originally not a sweep of calf against calf, but began with a sharp blow of Tori's heel at the bottom of Uke's calf so that the leg was partially paralysed, and Uke easier to throw. Many of the throwing techniques had atemi introductions to the main throw.

In 1882 Kano opened his school with nine pupils in Eshoji Temple, though it was not until three years later that he finally codified his system. He called his school Kodokan Judo, Judo meaning the Gentle Way and Kodokan meaning a Hall for Studying the Way. He brought the two words together specifically to differentiate his system from other schools which had already adopted the name Judo. (The term Judo had been used by the Kitoryu in 1830.) Kodokan Judo was very successful in a short space of time. There were competitions with other Ju-Jitsu schools, some of which the Kodokan won, and some it lost, but because of Kano's moral approach and academic (and thus 'respectable') status, he was rapidly given official support. At that point, many Ju-Jitsu men joined the Judo movement, took a rapid training in Judo and then became teachers within the schools where Judo training was becoming compulsory. The fact that Dr Kano was for many years one of the advisers to the Japanese Ministry of Education aided the spread of Judo in Japan enormously.

The 1890s and the turn of the century saw Judo travelling abroad. There is an account of Jigoro Kano himself facing an enormous Russian wrestler on a voyage to Europe. Standing just five feet four inches, Kano surprised the spectators, who expected his speedy defeat, by throwing his opponent with ease with a Koshi-Nage – and saved the Russian's head from a nasty knock on the deck by placing his hand underneath as the man fell.

By the 1920s and 1930s, Kano was travelling abroad regularly – he made his first trip to the Budokwai in London in 1920 and was still active and alert in 1935 when T. P. Leggett met him for the first time.

> He came over here with Takasaki and Kotani [remembers Mr Leggett]. He was very impressive. Even in old age he had this marvellous posture and his English was perfect, academic, but very good. He was the headmaster of two of the main colleges of Japan – the founding of Judo was only one side of him. In fact, he had a first-rate brain and he was a highly cultured man. Not moderately cultured – highly cultured. He knew more about European history than most of us.

Kano worked ceaselessly for the furtherance of Judo and it was a reflection of his success that Judo was a subject of discussion *vis-à-vis* the Olympic Games as early as the 1930s. But Kano himself had mixed views. In a meeting with Gunji Koizumi, founder of British Judo in 1936, he described his attitude as 'passive'. In the *Budokwai Quarterly Bulletin*, April 1947, Mr Koizumi reported Kano's precise statement:

> I do not feel inclined to take any initiative. For one thing, Judo in reality is not a mere sport or game. I regard it as a principle of life, art, science. In fact, it is a means for personal cultural attainment.

He went on to say that he was concerned about the intro-duction of the element of nationalism and felt strongly that

> Contest Judo was a retrograde form. Judo should be free, as art and science, from any external influences, political,

national, racial, financial or any other organised interest . . .
Judo, itself, is held by us all in a position at the high altar.
To reconcile this point of view with the Western idea is
difficult. Success or the satisfactory result of joining the
Olympic Games would much depend on the degree of
understanding of Judo by other participating countries.

Kano died in 1938 well before the Olympics issue was settled,
and also before the founding of the International Judo Federation (1952) which he regarded as far more important. But he
stands as one of the great educational innovators of the twentieth century, as his ideas have attained universal recognition.

The history of Judo in Britain

The history of the martial arts in Japan is punctuated by outstanding individual figures. The major movements, the major
developments, have always stemmed from one person who
combined the qualities of a superlative technician with the
charisma of a leader. Always the Ryu or schools continued to
exist while there existed one person able to assume the role of
leader, or while there was a central organization strong enough
to fulfil that function. After that, the school was consigned to
history. But at the same time there were breakaway groups,
some bona fide and well-meaning, some just well-meaning and
some neither. While the martial arts were still being tested in
battle, the matter was often settled conclusively – the theories
which did not work died with their proponents. When the
martial arts (Bujutsu) became the martial ways (Budo) the
problems of really testing theories and masters became more
complex. It is no doubt a reflection on the complexity of the
world of martial arts that there have always been conflicting
ideas and therefore conflicting schools in Japan and the East in
general.

The history of Judo in Britain and, in fact, every other Western
country where it has taken root, has followed the same pattern.

There are reliable but slightly different organizations, and some which leave a lot to be desired. But in much the same way as in Japan, Judo developed in this country through the influence of certain individuals, in particular four Japanese whose characters made an indelible impression upon British Judo in its most formative stage: Gunji Koizumi, Yukio Tani, Kenshiro Abe and Masutaro O-Tani.

It is fitting that one of the first and one of the greatest exponents of Ju-Jitsu ever to be seen in this country should also have been one of the seminal figures in the development of British Judo. Yukio Tani (1881–1950) was only eighteen when he was brought to this country by Barton Wright, an entrepreneur who had seen Tani fight in Japan and had realized the dramatic potential. Tani had studied in the Shin-no-Shinto-Ryu and, though physically small, was an extremely able contestman, having been one of the stars of the Doshisha University. In Britain, he toured the music halls offering £100 to anyone who could beat him, and within a short time he became very famous. It is Tani who was the origin of the 'Jap' wrestler in George Bernard Shaw's Major Barbara who armlocked Todger Fairmile. One of Tani's favourite moves was a kind of flying double-armlock: when the huge, strong wrestlers used to approach him with arms outstretched, Tani would catch the wrists, jump up with both feet on their shoulders and put on a double armlock which invariably came as a great surprise to the wrestlers.

No one who ever fought with him could doubt his immense contest ability. Hackenschmidt, the unassailable catch-as-catch-can champion wrestler, once told Marcus Kaye, 5th Dan and President of the Budokwai for many years, that he always studiously avoided meeting Yukio Tani in contest conditions.

In fact, only once was Tani beaten in a formal challenge during his music hall days, and that was by another Japanese Ju-Jitsu man. A rival entrepreneur brought over Taro Miyake, a younger and highly trained Ju-Jitsu exponent and in the classic encounter which took place in the Tivoli Theatre, London, scene of Tani's many triumphs, Miyake won. It was characteristic of both men that Tani and Miyake went on to write the first English book on the subject, *The Game of Ju-Jitsu*, and set up the first Ju-Jitsu school in Britain at 305 Oxford Street, London.

However, even on his tours in the early years of this century, Tani taught occasionally. One of his pupils was his manager Barton Wright who later claimed to have developed a system of his own called Bartitsu (with which Sherlock Holmes is supposed to have overcome Moriarty, though Watson describes it incorrectly as Baritsu). Marcus Kaye, who was one of the first British Dan Grades (and a celebrated figure in his own right, having effected a daring escape from a German prisoner of war camp in World War I), received his first lessons from a man who was for a time Mr Tani's dresser in the music halls – and who charged four guineas for twelve lessons (in 1920)!

Tani also studied Judo in Japan, but as he himself said once to T. P. Leggett, one his most celebrated pupils: 'I am a good third-class Judo man, but against boxers, wrestlers and savate-men I have perhaps unrivalled experience.'

It was because of Tani's speed and skill, particularly on the ground, and his ability to overcome much bigger men that the legends of secret pressure points developed, and it was only with the founding of the Budokwai in 1918 that formal Judo training became available for the first time. The Budokwai – The Society for Martial Ways – was founded at 15 Lower Grosvenor Place, London, SW1, by another charismatic figure, Gunji Koizumi, widely known as G.K.

Born in 1885, Koizumi first studied Ken-jutsu at the age of twelve and then Ju-Jitsu at the Tenjin Shin-Yo Ryu though he actually learned his Judo in Singapore. An engineer by training, he, like Kano, was a widely educated man, not only running a business in Japanese and Chinese art, but becoming one of the leading experts in Japanese and Chinese lacquer. In fact, it was Koizumi who was called in to advise on the 1936 Chinese Art exhibition and repaired some of the exhibits chipped in transit. It was also Koizumi who did much work to organize the Victoria and Albert lacquer collection.

Koizumi was a deeply thinking man and regarded Judo in much the same light as Dr Kano himself – hence the mutual respect that existed between the two following Kano's various visits to England. Following upon his founding of the Budokwai in 1918 Koizumi was later to be instrumental not only in developing European Judo, taking British teams abroad, but also founding the British Judo Association and the European Judo Union, which led directly to the International Judo Federation. Koizumi, therefore, played a crucial role in the growth of Judo internationally as well as Judo in Britain.

Koizumi's Judo, while not of the contest standard of Tani (whom he appointed chief instructor) was stylistically pure. He based his Judo thinking on the dynamic principles with which he was familiar through his engineering background, but at the same time Judo was very much a method of character training for him.

> Mental and spiritual balance depends upon clearness of conscience, absence of prejudice and its stability depends on independence of thought and conviction, – just as stability of body-balance depends on independence of external support [he wrote in a Budokwai newsletter in the 1940s]. The theory of Judo, like food, to be of any benefit must become an integral part of one's natural self [he wrote in another].

The series of penetrating articles contained in the Budokwai journal over the years on Mental Judo, the Aesthetics of Judo, the Master Mind, Non-Resistance as well as numerous pieces on specific Judo techniques, indicate clearly Koizumi's complete approach to Judo.

Koizumi and Tani provided a perfectly balanced base for the development of Judo in Britain. If Koizumi, President of the Budokwai from its formation to his death in 1965, was the idealist, Tani was the traditionalist. Tani, who was formally a 4th Dan in Judo, would repeat 'You learn by suffering', yet as Chief Instructor of the Budokwai until his retirement in 1937 following a stroke, he maintained a very acute awareness of the needs of his pupils – though he could be very tough indeed.

Kaye recounts how one day a Dan Grade asked Tani to let him see what 'a real contest' with Tani would be like, Tani obliged with a short full-out assault and describing afterwards the 'dizzy' thirty seconds, the Dan Grade said he was 'terrified, but better informed'.

Tani's retirement from practice in 1937 brought to an end the close partnership established with Koizumi. Though very different personalities, they were renowned not just for the training sessions at Lower Grosvenor Place, but also for their performance of Kata in public demonstrations, particularly Kime-no-Kata. Though once rich from his touring days, Tani never considered wealth of any importance and money would slip through his fingers. He died in 1950.

Mr Koizumi, however, enjoyed better health and was still on the mat in his eightieth year, though his eyesight was gradually failing. He guided the expansion of European Judo (he took the first British team to Germany in 1929 and many teams subsequently as well as running courses in Austria, Germany, Switzerland and the USA, as well as in the UK) and he controlled the growth of the Budokwai, which moved from Lower Grosvenor Place to GK House, 4 Gilston Road, London SW10, in 1954. By April 1965 he felt he had done all he could for Judo and to avoid suffering from serious deterioration of health he preferred to leave this life quietly and with dignity. On 15 April he took his own life. He was posthumously raised to 8th Dan by the Kodokan.

The passing of Tani and Koizumi brought to an end the first chapter in the history of Judo in Britain, but by the mid-1960s the Judo world was very different to those fresh, enthusiastic pre-war days. Despite the skill of both, no two men could hope satisfactorily to convey a complex and rich skill that is Judo, and the seeds for technical expansion – both in training and individual techniques – were sewn by sending able and promising British Judoka to train at the Kodokan in Japan.

The first British Judoka to be sent to Tokyo was Trevor Leggett, then an eighteen-year-old 3rd Dan. He had originally wanted to become a concert pianist, but was forbidden by his father and 'on the rebound' took up Judo. He started in 1932 and within fifteen months, having trained every night, achieved his 1st Dan while at the same time studying for a degree in law at the University of London. He travelled to Europe to study Judo and, in 1938, was sent to Japan. He would practise at one of the university Dojos at lunch-time for an hour, and then change and go to the Kodokan and start again at 4 p.m. for about three hours. He would also have private lessons, so that most days he would practise for about five hours. At the same time he studied Japanese for two or three hours a day. He learned a greater variety of techniques – including Uchi-Mata and Maki-Komi which have since become very important contest throws – and differing training methods. But he remembers, too, that Judo was much rougher in the pre-war days than now. In 1941, after Pearl Harbor, Leggett was interned with other Embassy staff, but continued practising Judo with his police guards. He was by now 5th Dan.

On his return to Britain in 1942, he was almost immediately transferred to India, and it was only in the post-War period that the experience gained in Japan began to have its effect on British Judo. From 1947 to 1957, Leggett taught at the Budokwai, holding special weekend classes for Dan Grades from all over the country, in an attempt to broaden the Judo which was being taught in the provinces as well as those based in London.

He insisted on keeping the Japanese names for throws at a time when there was much pressure to anglicize Judo language, and he introduced the traditional Japanese practice of more arduous summer and winter training sessions.

His position as Head of the Japanese Service for the BBC took him frequently to Japan, and he was thus instrumental in maintaining the close contact with the Kodokan which has directly benefited the development of British Judo. He resumed the tradition of sending the most promising British Dan Grades to

the Kodokan for further study (which he himself had inaug-
urated) not just to learn Judo but to learn to read and write
Japanese as well – he wanted Judo and Judoka to be associated
with culture as well as sport. He was also instrumental in bringing over to England many highly skilled Japanese Judoka as
instructors, including Kisaburo Watanabe. Always an individual
and somewhat solitary person, he founded the Renshuden in
North London as a centre for serious brown and black belts, but
in 1964, he stopped practising, feeling he could no longer
demonstrate to the standard he required. He had then attained
8th Dan, at the time the highest grade ever given to a non-
Japanese. Apart from his teaching and his personal example,
Leggett has made a major contribution to British Judo with his
series of technical Judo books and his more philosophical
volumes, including *Zen and the Ways* (Routledge & Kegan Paul).
He is now a leading translator of Japanese and Sanskrit texts.

By the time Leggett retired Judo had been transformed from
the more intimate coterie it was when he started. Through the
1950s and 1960s, there was an extraordinary world-wide expansion which was very much reflected in this country. In 1947
there were over forty clubs affiliated to the Budokwai and there
was clearly a need for a national organization. In January 1948
the British Judo Association was formed and many clubs joined.
Apart from generally overseeing the Judo movement, the BJA
was to select national teams to contest abroad, as well as run
national tournaments. Two years later the inevitable occurred.
Pat Butler, a former treasurer of the BJA, decided to form his
own national group, the Amateur Judo Association.

The 1950s also saw the founding of another national organization, the British Judo Council. The BJC was – and still is –
unusual in that it was the only British national group ever to be
founded as much upon a set of philosophical principles as the
inspiration of one man. Kenshiro Abe, born in the Tokushima
province in 1916, became a very able Judoka at a young age.
Starting Judo in 1930 at the age of fourteen, he was awarded his
2nd Dan a year later from the Butokukwai – the national martial

arts organization. At eighteen he was awarded 5th Dan from the Butokukwai, the youngest Judoka ever to hold the grade. In his fighting career he won a number of major championships, including the East Japan versus West Japan contest, and the 5th Dan championships held in the Emperor's Palace.

From a young age, Kenshiro Abe regarded the martial arts as expressions of deeper ideas – significantly, he was strongly influenced by personal contact with Morihei Ueshiba, the founder of Aikido. And though Abe also studied Aikido, Kendo and Jukendo (The Way of the Bayonet) and during the late 1930s taught at the Special Judo College of the Butokukwai in Kyoto, he was gradually forming his own philosophy which he later called Kyu-Shin-Do.

In 1938 he was promoted to 6th Dan, the youngest in Japan, and in 1945 7th Dan. He became chief instructor of Doshisa University (the same university, incidentally which Tani represented nearly fifty years before) as well as the instructor for the Kyoto Police.

In 1955 he came from the Kodokan to England at the invitation of the London Judo Society, a South London Club, but a year later left to form his own school.

Strongly independent and even unpredictable to the point of eccentricity as a person, Kenshiro Abe was nevertheless regarded with great respect as a Judoka and as an instructor and the BJC attracted thousands of members fairly quickly.

He was, however, certainly something of an enigma. He possessed very definite and uncompromising ideas about life in general and Judo in particular. For instance, after years of thought and study, he approached the breaking of the balance in Judo in a greatly simplified way to the standard Kodokan manner (see chapter 3) and his system remains controversial. At other times, however, he would go to the extremes of complexity, breaking down a throw into as many as fifteen or more component parts in an exhaustive analysis.

His courses often involved long lectures and hard, concentrated periods of training – but then he would take the Judokas out to a local playground to the swings or do Aikido moves in a sandpit. Many English Judoka were bewildered by this kind of unpredictability, yet he maintained respect not least because his own Judo was very light and very fast.

There were other sides to him too – during his years at 10 Stuart Road, Acton, the home of Masutaro O-Tani and for years the centre of the BJC, he transformed the garden into a carefully nurtured Japanese garden.

Kyu-Shin-Do was the central statement for Abe's personal approach to Judo. Loosely translated, it means the Seeker's Way to the Essence of Things, or the Truth. He felt there were three fundamental principles within Kyu-Shin-Do which should be reflected both in the Judoka's Judo and in his outside life:

1 That all things throughout the universe are in a constant state of motion (Banbutsu Ruten).
2 This motion is rhythmic and flowing (Ritsu Do).
3 All things work and flow in perfect harmony (Chowa).

One of the essential practical expressions of Kenshiro Abe's Kyu-Shin-Do was that it was not enough to win at any cost. Success in contest, he felt, was only important in that it demonstrated superior skill. This approach was fundamental to the whole concept of Judo in its pure form, but it was not a popular approach at a time when the Olympics was making its influence felt, and Abe encountered considerable opposition over these and other points.

In 1960 Abe was badly injured in a car accident and four years later, still not fully recovered, he returned to Japan. His place as the active leader of the BJC was taken by another Japanese figure, Masutaro O-Tani (1898–1977).

Born in Nagasaki, O-Tani came to England in 1919 and resumed his Judo training (begun in Japan) at the Budokwai in 1921. He worked hard to overcome his small stature, and he became a trainee assistant to Yukio Tani, and from 1927 to 1932 was instructor at Oxford and Cambridge Universities. In 1932 he became the instructor at the Anglo-Japanese Club and then, when the club was destroyed during the war, began teaching the Home Guard and the Territorial Army. It was while teaching the Metropolitan Police that he was given the nickname 'Smiler' – because he always smiled.

In 1954, he founded the Masutaro O-Tani Society of Judo, but began working with the BJC in 1958. In 1959 Abe, himself then 8th Dan, personally awarded him a 7th Dan. In 1969, when Abe returned briefly to Britain, he promoted O-Tani to 8th Dan. A year later, the MOSJ formally amalgamated with the BJC.

Throughout the 1970s until his death in 1977, O-Tani proved a popular, active figure, visiting clubs, taking courses, expanding the BJC and being known generally for his etiquette and courteousness. Until he was well into his fifties, he had continued doing energetic Nage-Waza, and even then he was noted for his speed of attack and control of balance which he had developed in his early Judo years to compensate for his small frame – he was just five foot in height. Even during his sixties, he was still formidable on the ground, with the same concentration of energy and the special quality of elusiveness that characterized the groundwork of his teacher, Yukio Tani.

The late 1950s and 1960s saw dramatic changes in Judo which became dominated by the possibility and then the reality, in 1964, of Judo becoming an Olympic sport. The changes, which resulted in Judo being transformed as a way of life envisaged by Kano and others to a sport, were gradual and perhaps inevitable. Though Judo originally contained leg-locks and wrist-locks, which allowed the small, fast man to compete with the large and the strong, the gradual elimination of these 'dangerous' techniques meant the inevitable introduction of weight categories. Welcomed by some and regarded as the end of Judo by others, they have become a lasting feature of the Judo scene. The introduction of Koka and Yuko and Wazaris too became necessary as competitions became more important – originally, there was only Ippon, one point.

The competitive emphasis brought other things too. It brought a greater popularity to Judo, not so much as a spectator sport, but as a participatory sport. The British Schools Judo Association was formed, with Judo being accepted within the school curriculum which, with successes at Olympic level, brought the activity of Judo to a much wider public. Britain also played an influential role in international Judo – Charles Palmer, 8th Dan, was for many years President of the International Judo Federation and the European Judo Union. In fact, it was largely due to the efforts of Mr Palmer that Judo was reinstated as an Olympic sport after being omitted from the 1968 Olympics. One of the first British Judokas to train at the Kodokan after the war, he has been equally active on the domestic front, having been President of the British Judo Association for many years, and sat on numerous national committees concerned both with Judo and general sports policies. A handful of British Judokas, many of whom had trained at the Budokwai, which is still the main centre for Olympic Judo training in the country, became well known. The number of Judo books available in English have also increased, with new titles coming on to the market each year.

But the development of Judo as sport rather than as art has also resulted in a period when etiquette and basic technique appeared to receive less emphasis in many clubs than contest technique. It has also meant that there are too many prospective pupils, both juniors and seniors, for the numbers of experienced Dan Grades to cope with satisfactorily – often classes are far too large for adequate safety margins, and too large for an acceptable level of skill to be maintained. The fierce competitive nature of Judo as sport has seemed to result in many more accidents coming not just from crowded mats but from techniques dangerously or forcibly applied. However, growing awareness of these problems may bring changes over the next decade.

Certainly, British Judo has come a long way from those days of a handful of Kyu grades in the Dojo of 15 Lower Grosvenor Place. The enthusiasm engendered there led to such startling events, however, as the establishment of a Judo class run by British prisoners of war in a German camp on a canvas made from storage bags stolen from the German stores.

There are now probably about 100,000 Judokas active to some degree in Britain, and the number is growing. The British Judo Association which retains the sole right to select a national team and receives the major government grants, continues to grow. And so does the next largest organization, the British Judo Council, which also has members teaching in schools, colleges and sports centres. And though the different organizations have their disagreements, past history indicates that it is no bad thing to have different organizations able to express different view-points.

In the final analysis, the success of any club and of any individual is dependent upon the technique and the personal example of the teacher concerned rather than on any fixed conception, duplicated thousands of times.

And Judo will change. Various throws have been through fashionable times until the next generation of Judokas learned to counter them out of existence, and then a new series of techniques would come into prominence. T. P. Leggett was told by a senior Japanese Judoka that because Westerners are not just taller than Japanese but different in proportion, certain techniques would be more applicable. Uchi-Mata was one, and so it has proved. Sumi-Gaeshi was another, but that has yet to have a great Western exponent. Such is the fascination and the endless appeal of Judo.

In its very early days, Judo was beset with the image of mystical pressure points and Oriental magic. Its more recent history has been dominated by medals and sport. Perhaps the next two or three decades will point the indicator towards a middle way. Who knows?

2 The art and etiquette of Judo

Art

Art in western society has been almost exclusively regarded in terms of an art object. It may be a piano sonata or a symphony, sculpture or painting, novel or play, but the importance is in the work of art itself. The artist, as much as his audience, is concerned with subjugating everything to his art because it is the work that will be judged by others, not himself.

However, in some societies, in the East, and particularly in China and Japan, this is only one aspect of art. Equally important is the fact that the individual can also develop a high level of skill in his actions in order to make a work of art out of himself – not for the admiration or the gratification of an audience, but for a deeper experience of his own life. It is interesting to note, also, that in Japanese society personal effort is more widely admired than talent because it is considered that only through mastering a skill after a long and hard struggle will the individual change and develop, enabling him to lead a far richer existence. In its essence, this is what makes Judo, Kendo, Aikido and the rest martial *arts*.

So, Judo is about personal change, personal development. That is one reason why it is called a Path or a Way. As we travel along it we change. We change physically. We become fitter and more flexible; we develop better posture and therefore our movements become less wild and more co-ordinated. When a White Belt is attacked, he often goes as stiff as a board. Everything stiffens, including his mind. When a more experienced Judoka is attacked, he doesn't remain immobile, but he only moves what he really needs to move.

We also change mentally. Our muscles and bodies move according to the dictates of our minds. At the beginning, in Judo, our minds are either in a state of shock, when attacked, or a state of confusion as we try to assimilate what are really complex techniques which themselves alter in thousands of tiny ways according to different situations, different partners. Through diligent training, however, Uchikomi, Randori, Kata, we can begin to sort out some of these mental confusions and achieve a greater clarity. Two things differentiate the advanced Judoka from the beginner: a clarity of mind and the ability to translate mental decisions into controlled action, creative action.

Dr Kano himself said on many occasions that the ultimate aim of Judo was to perfect the individual to enable him to contribute to the welfare of mankind as a whole. He regarded himself as an educator in the broadest sense of the word, and one of his slogans was 'Mutual Welfare and Benefit'. He taught repeatedly that the lessons learned in the Dojo should be applied to the everyday life of the Judoka and, at its highest, Judo was a training for life.

In other words, Judo is not something that takes place just within a Dojo, but should be present within the Judoka at all times. All the difficulties that present themselves during the course of the day should be regarded as opportunities for furthering one's Judo mind and Judo body. To take a mundane example such as carrying suitcases up a few flights of stairs. One can either lug them up reluctantly, and nothing is learned, or one can approach the task with vigour and, by concentrating on posture and relaxed but controlled movements, contribute to one's Judo training.

Much the same approach can be used during meetings with difficult people and a whole host of tasks and problems which we dread. Gradually one learns to transcend the petty details that dog so much of our lives. Everything should be regarded as a preparation for something else, for a higher vision of ourselves.

In common with other art forms, Judo demands a high level of technical skill. To turn fast and with great accuracy, to remain very sensitive to your partner's movements and to capitalize on his weaknesses requires constant practice, and certainly a daily practice – it can be demoralizing to see how quickly the finely-honed edge of a top Judoka becomes blunt with a few non-active days.

Naturally, repetition can and does become tiresome, but repetition is the only way to make certain basic movements second nature. It is necessary, therefore, to think beyond the daily stretching and technical exercises to maintain the feeling for the creative side of Judo. It is after all the element of personal creativity that makes Judo an art. If we are not constantly working at new techniques, new combinations, trying to look at old techniques with new eyes in order to improve and develop, then staleness will inevitably set in. The fascination of Judo, and the depth within it, lies often in the tiny details – that a little finger raised a fraction means the difference between a knock-down technique and a full throw, and the movement of a foot one inch to one side is the difference between an insecure and a firm hold.

From its conception, Judo was regarded as a physical, mental and spiritual training, and, strictly speaking, the grade a Judoka wears should denote a level attained in all three aspects. Sadly, only too often it marks purely a physical achievement. But in many ways, the Judokas themselves are the losers – until they come to teach and begin to influence others.

One of the most enjoyable and satisfying experiences in Judo comes when working with a partner of similar attitude; the concentration, the creative moves, counters and combinations involve the two people in a deep and absorbing Randori where physical limitations are forgotten and time seems to stand still. When this happens, one feels a sense of uplift, and penetrating clarity because the total self is involved in an artistic expression of the highest quality. This is Judo as art. Compare that to two participants in a contest spending most of their time fighting for grips and being satisfied to end the contest with a small knock-down technique. The harmony is nil and the standard of creative technique is poor. Here the emphasis is on brute strength and the crude formula of a winner and a loser.

This is not to decry the importance of competition. Those who practise Judo as an art should have no reservations in entering competitions dominated by sportsmen. Superior technique should prevail, and if it doesn't, more practice is required. It is as simple as that. It is the superior technique and the creative imagination needed to produce it that is important, not winning or losing. The impromptu laps of 'honour' or the brandishing of a fist to the audience after a successful hold down degrades Judo. Success in individual competitions means little when compared to a higher aim of self-development that a true interpretation of Judo entails. It is because of this almost intro-verted nature of Judo that it has never succeeded as a spectator event on a broad-based level. Judo is for the participants and those watching who have a substantial idea of the intricacies, and not really for a general audience waiting to be stimulated by human combat.

There are certain Japanese expressions which pinpoint con-cepts worth considering and which enable the Judoka to ap-preciate a deeper perspective within martial arts. Shin means 'heart', both in the sense of essence and emotion; it is the central psychological state of mental poise. Someone who possesses a pure Shin can momentarily lose that purity, but can regain it fairly quickly. To attain a true state of Shin is difficult – traditionally, Zen monks spend years doing this. Ki, on the other hand, is energy – energy in a psycho-physical sense. When a small Judoka throws a larger partner in a contest, Ki is likely to be present. It is not technique, nor is it strength; rather it is the concentration of all the energy in the body to that one total action. For that one moment, the Judoka feels suffused with unlimited energy or a 'cosmic current'. It is important to note, however, that the experience of Ki should also exist when sitting still or performing ordinary movements.*

In his classic book, *Zen in the Art of Archery* (Routledge & Kegan Paul), Eugen Herrigel relates one story of a man who approached a Japanese master of fencing and asked to be taught. The fencing master looked at the prospective student carefully and said that he didn't believe that the student was a beginner. The student replied that he had no knowledge of sword technique at all. It was only later, after further questioning, that the student admitted that he had, as a youth, struggled within himself to overcome the fear of death. Could this be what the swordmaster saw? Yes, the swordmaster said and added: 'You need no technical training, you are already a master.'

So, neither Shin nor Ki are just concepts, but realities that can be demonstrated and recognized by others.

The same applies to Ri and Ji. Ji refers to the techniques themselves as the concrete heritage of experiences and lessons learned by masters of the past. Ri is the real feeling of those techniques. To a certain extent, Ji can be taught by someone to someone, but Ri can arise only through the direct experience of the student himself. Leggett uses a good analogy to differentiate between the two in *Zen and the Ways*. When one is learning a foreign language and one can translate sentences in one's head and reply to questions, that is Ji; when one replies instinctively, that is Ri. It is a useful experience to ask oneself in how many of our own techniques does Ri really exist?

Finally, Isshin and Zanshin. Isshin means to commit oneself completely to an action while Zanshin means to hold something in reserve. Though it appears paradoxical to utilize both, they have their places within the performance of a technique. When attempting to throw, we cannot contemplate failure if we are really intent on bringing it off. On the other hand, if we don't have a deeper reserve on which we can draw should

* A lengthier and more precise discussion of these expressions are contained in Trevor Leggett's *Zen and the Ways* (Routledge & Kegan Paul).

the technique fail, then we are in an extremely vulnerable state.

All these concepts can be appreciated on many levels and will often mean something, even to a beginner. By the time that the beginner starts moving through the Dan Grades, however, his understanding of the concepts will have been broadened by experience. It is the depth of experience acquired only through years of practice which is why traditionally the Japanese regard 1st Dan merely as marking the end of the apprenticeship period, not as an end in itself.

The development of the more subtle parts of ourselves in the martial arts has been beautifully and concisely put by the greatest of Japanese swordmasters, Miyamoto Musashi. In *A Book of Five Rings* (the Go Rin Sho No),* where Mushashi distils sixty years experience, he discusses spiritual bearing in strategy. (Strategy for Musashi means both formal combat and the struggle for personal development.)

> In strategy, your spiritual bearing must not be any different from normal. Both in fighting and everyday life, you should be determined though calm. Meet the situation without tenseness, yet not recklessly, your spirit settled yet unbiased. Even when your spirit is relaxed, do not let your body relax, and when your body is relaxed, do not let your spirit slacken. Do not let your spirit be influenced by your body, or your body be influenced by your spirit. Be neither in-sufficiently spirited nor over spirited. An elevated spirit is weak and a low spirit is weak. Do not let the enemy see your spirit.
>
> Small people must be completely familiar with the spirit of large people, and large people must be familiar with the

* *A Book of Five Rings* by Musashi, translated by Victor Harris and published by Allison & Buzby, 1974. Musashi looks at the various aspects of strategy in five books written during a period of intense meditation in a cave in 1645, towards the end of his life. The five books are: 'The Ground Book', 'The Water Book', 'The Fire Book', 'The Wind Book', 'The Book of the Void'.

23

spirit of small people. Whatever your size, do not be misled by the reactions of your body. With your spirit open and unconstricted, look at things from a high point of view. You must cultivate your wisdom and spirit. Polish your wisdom: learn public justice, distinguish between good and evil, study the Ways of different arts one by one. When you cannot be deceived by men, you will have realised the wisdom of strategy.

The wisdom of strategy is different from other things. On the battlefield, even when you are hard-pressed, you should ceaselessly research the principles of strategy so that you can develop a steady spirit.

This crucial passage comes from the second of The Five Rings, 'The Water Book', and contains a wealth of important points for the practising Judoka. Each of the short sentences, Musashi himself advises, should not just be read, memorized or imitated, but deeply absorbed and applied. The first two lines can be taken as an example.

In strategy, your spiritual bearing must not be any different from normal. Both in fighting and everyday life, you should be determined though calm.

Musashi indicates that even under the greatest stresses, the behaviour, technique and bearing must be clear as pure water, untroubled, free-flowing, moving smoothly around or over apparently insuperable obstacles.

The analogy can be extended even further. If a river comes to an obstacle which it cannot surmount, or bypass, it gradually accumulates until eventually it succeeds in overcoming the obstacle and can continue on its way. Similarly, if we find there is one person with whom we practise who is too skilled or too stiff or apparently too big for us to overcome, continuous thought and practice will bring success in the end. Kazuzo Kudo, in his book *Judo in Action* (Japan Publications Trading Company), explains the introduction of Kata Guruma into Judo.

24

He reports that while Dr Kano was still practising Ju-Jitsu, there was one colleague whom he could never overcome, Fukushima, a large but also a skilled man. Only after days of study, poring through old martial arts texts, and weeks of practice did Dr Kano arrive at Kata Guruma and successfully apply the technique to Fukushima.

To return to those two sentences in 'The Water Book'. It is important not to overlook the second main point made by Musashi. In both sentences he stresses that one's bearing in fighting and everyday life must be the same. In other words, the swordsman, or in our case the Judoka, must strive to bring his everyday life up to the standard of his Judo personality and technical level. Even those who regard Judo as a sport feel that there is something special in the activity, the atmosphere and the environment, something which is not present outside the Dojo. They themselves feel different within a Dojo and regret that they do not feel the same outside. But Musashi exhorts his readers to maintain the same attitudes, whether in business or when walking down the street. To take a mundane example: few Judoka would yell at someone in anger in a Dojo, or try to win a contest with a concealed and dangerous technique which sets out to injure his partner; the same should apply in all other aspects of life.

Naturally, it is a difficult ideal to live up to, but that is one reason why the true Judoka does not stop learning once his contesting days are over. The Judoka who passes the age of fighting should not suddenly feel relegated to a secondary position as teacher or Kata exponent. He is still learning to apply those highest ideals, learning through teaching, learning through Kata, learning for life. When Judo is regarded in this manner, it is often the most difficult, but the most rewarding and stimulating part of the Way. No longer is the Judoka stimulated to practise hard and well by the warning of the next competition; instead, he has to search within himself for a different and deeper stimulus, which leads to a far more profound and enriching experience. Eastern and Western artistic and philosophic traditions point to the fact that this is the greatest contest of all.

Much that is written about the martial arts in general is guilty of exaggeration and over-mystification. Some of the claims made would be amusing were they not to influence unsuspecting readers with overblown imaginations.

But there is a mystery inherent in the martial arts. When a person has trained diligently in the physical, mental and spiritual aspects of his art, and when he has begun to acquire the freedom from physical and mental fear and attained a certain unshakeable poise noticeable in all his actions, he becomes, in a sense, greater than the sum of his parts. This is where the mystery of the martial arts lies. This is the real goal attainable, to some extent, by all who follow the path in a disciplined, methodical and imaginative manner. This is what makes Judo not just a sport, nor just a form of self-defence, but an art form in its own right, and the practitioner an artist.

Etiquette

The etiquette of Judo has often been criticized by Western Judoka as an over-elaborate and out-dated system of Oriental manners quite inappropriate to the Western environment. What has been overlooked, however, is that the Japanese are an immensely practical people, and the ritual that exists does so for more than simply decorous reasons.

At its best, Judo is a martial art, and as such can involve raw emotions of annoyance, anger and hatred. In fact, one of the purposes of pursuing a martial art is to refine these emotions and re-channel them to more effective expression. Yet the line between a Judo contest and a brawl can, at times, appear very thin, at least to an untutored eye. What is more important is that sometimes the participants themselves can be somewhat unsure of where that line is to be drawn. In a sense, it is through the nature of the etiquette involved that the spirit of Judo can be seen and expressed.

When two Judokas bow to each other before Randori or contest, they are first and foremost acknowledging that the forthcoming practice is for the benefit of both. The aim is not to injure or to trick your partner, but to raise the level of Judo. It is out of respect and consideration for one's partner that one enters a Dojo only with a clean body and a clean Judogi, and it is with the same feeling of respect that one bows.

The Rei has also an important personal aspect. This is the moment when one concentrates one's thoughts, harnesses and controls any trace of nerves in order to achieve an alert calm; one uses the physical act of bowing not to 'psyche' oneself up, but to develop a piercing determination to attain complete commitment. The Rei at the conclusion of the practice also has a dual function, thanking your partner for the practice and calming oneself down. The concluding Rei should have the added function of wiping out any unpleasantness that may have occurred during the Randori or contest: there is no point in carrying negative thoughts away from the mat.

The etiquette of Judo extends far beyond a bow before and after each practice. Etiquette suffuses every aspect of Judo, is part of the harmony of Judo and contributes enormously to the special atmosphere within a Dojo.

The art of Judo is acknowledged as one enters a Dojo. Instead of just opening the door and rushing in, it is of practical value to pause a moment and bow. It provides the Judoka with a moment's space to discard the frustrations and exhilarations of the ordinary world, the business or domestic problems and the general worries which disturb our inner harmony.

The Rei on entering the Dojo offers the opportunity to turn one's mind completely to Judo and to the best in oneself. But the Rei is also a gesture of humility; it states to oneself that one is coming to the Dojo to learn; curiously, perhaps, the mere act of bowing on entering the Dojo when done properly helps to create a greater state of receptivity in oneself. One can achieve a mental state where one is less likely to show off, for instance, or less likely to become frustrated and angry at one's own failures.

Such quietening on entering and when bowing before stepping on to the mat is important, not least during those 'grey' periods when nothing one tries seems to work, and no progress seems to be made. In many ways, it is worth regarding those grey periods as exciting ones, because often they herald a major breakthrough – if only we had the vision to see a little into the future. So, the Rei as one enters and leaves the Dojo, as one steps on and off the Tatami, lends an evenness to one's practice, so that one does not become too elated at times of rapid progress and too depressed at times of apparent stasis.

The etiquette of Judo also involves the respect junior grades show for the senior grades, and, equally important, the respect the senior grades show for their juniors. A senior grade should

Tachi-Rei, Zarei. The Rei is much more than just an antiquated system of Oriental manners. It is a time to acknowledge one's partner and concentrate and quieten oneself

never 'paste' a junior grade around a mat for some imagined slight. If a Green Belt has managed to throw a Dan Grade, the Green Belt should be congratulated, not punished. After all, hopefully, the Dan Grade has learnt an important lesson, having been shown one of his weaknesses. He should be grateful, not angry. When practising Randori with a junior grade, the senior grade must not be afraid to 'lose face' and allow himself to be thrown. If the junior grade has worked hard and well and managed three-quarters of a throw, surely, in a Randori, his partner can help him with the final quarter. That is what teaching is all about. On the other hand, it only hinders the junior grade if the senior grade makes it too easy.

In a word, etiquette implies concern, concern to bring the best out of your partners, students and yourself, both in the Dojo and in everyday life. Without etiquette Judo would be in danger of becoming a system for thugs and would not be Judo.

Note: The standing Rei must be done with the heels together, men placing hands at the sides and women hands in front above the knees. The bow is made from the hips. The kneeling Rei is done as follows: left knee down first and toes turned under, then on to right knee, toes turned under. Toes are then straightened and crossed. Men should have the knees about a shoulder-width apart and women knees together. Left hand to the Tatami, then right, and touch the forehead lightly to the hands and then straighten up. Rise by reversing the procedure, maintaining good posture at all times. A more popular form of kneeling bow is to place both hands on the mat together.

In Randori and contest, you face a partner approximately six to ten feet apart and Rei before and after – each time one practises.

The Rei is made on entering and leaving the Dojo and on stepping on and off the mat. The Judoka should not step on or off the Tatami without having asked the senior instructor.

A Judo session should begin and end formally with a full kneeling Rei to the senior instructor.

3 The practice of Judo

Posture

Creative Judo springs from perfect posture. Without the poise and balance that is acquired from a good posture, the Judoka is unsteady on his feet and unsure and awkward in his movements. His freedom of action, the possibilities open to him to move left or right, forward or backward, are severely limited. That is why it is impossible to over-stress the importance of good posture from the beginning of a Judo career and to continue to observe and correct posture throughout each practice session. Bad posture acquired at the beginning of a Judo career is difficult to change later when bad habits have become ingrained in the performance of techniques, whereas attention paid to posture right at the start pays enormous dividends later on. This applies as much to groundwork as standing techniques.

The Judoka should stand upright, the feet about a shoulder-width apart, the body weight coming forwards slightly towards the toes. The knees should not be stiff but slightly flexed, as also the hips. The arms, when taking normal grip, should be loose, not stiff, with the elbows below the level of the hand. The hand grip itself should start from the little finger of each hand, curling the fingers inward; the wrist must remain flexible. The head should be upright and the eyes taking in a general view of the partner.

Traditional Japanese attitudes towards posture are centred on the Tanden, a point of strength located two inches beneath the navel. In all the martial arts, all movements stem from this point; in Japan, all movements, walking, sitting, standing, etc, stem from the Tanden. Development of awareness of this area brings the centre of gravity of the body down to a low point, so that the Judoka becomes difficult to unbalance and, traditionally, the Japanese regard awareness of Tanden as much a psychological as a physical grounding. Westerners, on the other hand, are generally too much orientated towards the upper body, particularly the shoulders and arms. They are, therefore, more prone to topple over, both psychologically and physically be-

Both Judoka here have sacrificed all traces of good posture, one in order to make some kind of throw or drag-down, the other in order not to be thrown. The likelihood, however, is that in this case, Uke will probably be put on his back anyway because he has tried to resist the technique rather than maintain his good posture and aim for a counter. This is a scrap – not Judo. It is difficult to achieve high standards all the time, particularly in the heat of a contest, but it is important to distinguish honestly when a technique has been a demonstration of Judo and when something quite different

Here, Tori's action is light and fast and based on balanced posture which is not always easy to achieve at the beginning, but which is not simply the preserve of the lighter Judoka. The practical advantages (the aesthetic benefits need not be enumerated) are that little strength is needed to throw, and if the movement has been mistimed, and Uke is able to step over the attacking right foot, Tori can attack again by a single movement of his right foot, and by drawing his left arm a little further through the circle

cause their centre is higher. So, a development of an awareness of the Tanden* is crucial to good posture.†

A light and confident natural posture means that you are always poised, ready to attack, avoid or counter at great speed. A heavy, dull posture means that your movement will inevitably be much slower. If you are stiff and pushing your

* A number of books discussing this point of centring describe it as the 'Hara' point, but generally, Hara refers to the principle, and Tanden to the point itself.
† A practice specifically designed to develop this awareness is clearly outlined in Trevor Leggett's *Zen and the Ways* (Routledge & Kegan Paul).

partner away with a strong-arm action in an attempt to prevent your partner attacking you, then you are also preventing yourself from attacking – as well as transmitting every move you make to your partner through your hand grip. When you finally decide to change the muscle action from defence to attack, this alteration is quickly picked up by your partner, who has then a chance to take evasive action.

If, on the other hand, your general posture is light, you will be able to make good use of your partner's movements in your attacking/countering action. Judo itself is a study of MOVE-MENT, not of strength. Strength is relative to each person and it is not a requirement of Judo to be strong. It is a requirement to be reasonably fit, and continuous practice of this martial art will make you fit whatever your physiological condition at the beginning.

When saying that Judo is a study of movement, it is necessary to emphasize that it is referring to the movement of two Judoka in action, and not just one person. There must be harmony in the movements of throwing and groundwork and not a clash of energy or strength in which the strongest wins. Not always will the most skilful person win: skill takes many years to acquire and develop and is particularly difficult to promote in a pre-dominantly strong-arm environment. But the dividends both in personal satisfaction and enjoyment, and in terms of sheer technique, are enormous – if the Judoka is prepared to take the trouble at the beginning of his career; or if he is prepared to change after some years of experience.

Judo is primarily concerned with developing oneself mentally and physically, transforming uncontrolled actions into con-trolled actions. To this end, we work with partners using competitive situations such as Randori or Shiai (contest) to bring out the best in ourselves. We try to beat our partners in a skilful way not, as the current trend suggests, using strength to over-power our partner. Winning by all costs should have little place in Judo: in those terms, it is easier to grab a stick and hit someone over the head. This is not to say that the skilful use of

The practice of Judo

natural strength is to be avoided. Quite the opposite. But the development of skill which stems from a firm posture should not be subordinated to strength just because skill requires more patience and practice.

A final word on posture: it is vital that whenever the natural posture is broken, either by one's own attacking action or by one's partner's, to return to Shizentai as soon as possible. Posture should not be allowed to deteriorate either when one is under a barrage of attacks, or when one is getting tired. It is at this stage that one's ability and technique needs to be at its best.

Negative and positive action

A negative action is one in which the end result of an action started comes to nothing. A positive action is one which achieves an end result, such as a throw scoring a full point (Ippon) or a counter-attack scoring a full point. It is not possible to achieve a good technique using negative thinking. There is a lot of negative Judo practised today where the Judoka is concerned purely with defensive action, pushing his partner away and using blocking actions to spoil his partner's technique. I do not know why, as there is so little personal satisfaction involved: defensive Judoka seem only interested in not losing rather than striving in a positive way to attack. This is a very common, but a very limited approach to Judo. On the other hand, positive Judo is much more satisfying, though perhaps more difficult in its initial stages, because it is unlimited in its scope.

If you attack your partner in a positive manner, using, for example, Ippon-Seoi-Nage (Single-arm shoulder throw) and your partner avoids, then your attack *becomes* negative. If your partner does nothing with the advantage he has gained by avoiding, then his action also becomes negative. If your partner uses his avoiding action to counter-attack whilst your posture is

35

weak and is successful, then his action is positive. In a good Judo contest, and also in normal practice (Randori), this interchange of negative/positive is continuous until one Judoka throws successfully. The same applies equally to groundwork.

A golden rule is: do not oppose force with force. When attacked, always avoid to counter, and think in a positive, creative way.

Harmony

The concept of harmony is the central principle of Judo. Strictly speaking, a Judo contest without harmony is a contradiction in terms: the contest becomes wrestling or unarmed combat or a brawl, but it is not Judo. A contest with harmony is a demonstration of a universal principle that 'Self and the Universe are in a body.' Dr Jigoro Kano always emphasized that the purpose of studying Judo was not to win contests or medals, but to perfect the body and mind for the benefit of society as a whole: 'Maximum efficient use of body and mind' and 'Mutual welfare and benefit' were two of Kano's most often-used sayings. And while the popularization of Judo in the West is undoubtedly of benefit, there is a danger that the transformation of Judo into a sport instead of a way of life will ultimately do Judo more harm than good. Increasingly in the West there is little evidence of harmony, either within the Dojo, or in the attitude of Judoka outside the Dojo.

It is important to note that Kano decided to concentrate on the principle of Ju (Gentleness or Yielding) in a manner that presupposed harmony simply because it was 'efficient', because it worked, and not just because it embodied a nice universal, not to say spiritual, concept. Ultimately, the simplest way to achieve mastery over an opponent was to blend with his actions and then assume control, not to meet force with force. Kano always acknowledged that it was not easy to attain the level of technique necessary to act in this way, but it was not his purpose to

By throwing yourself on to your knees, you ensure that you get low enough, but, apart from ending up in hospital eventually for knee operations, it restricts the opportunity for combinations or a rapid exit if the technique has been mistimed

provide an easy road – after all, he was aiming at self-perfection of the individual.

All the traditional techniques of Judo illustrate and use the principle of harmony: it is in the execution of those techniques that harmony is only too frequently lost. An example is the power-strength technique used in an attempted Morote-Seoi-Nage, when Tori (the thrower) attempts to use his arm and shoulder strength to swing his opponent onto his back in the same way that a novice (not an expert!) coal merchant would swing a sack of coal. A second, often-used approach to the same throw is for Tori to throw himself either on his knees or on his side regardless of what his partner is doing, but hoping that the sheer force of the movement will prevail. In both these examples the principle of harmony does simply not exist.

37

Now, an example of the same technique, Morote-Seoi-Nage, executed using the principle of harmony. Uke steps to his left with one step and Tori, who has stepped with Uke (the receiver), feels a second, similar step is about to be taken.

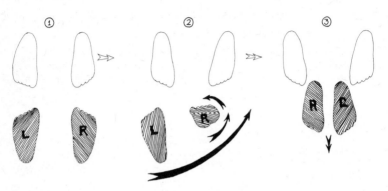

This kind of stepping movement works with a host of throws and therefore should be practised until it is absolutely second nature.

Instead of repeating his step, Tori pivots on his right foot and aims for a Morote position. This move is immensely simple but remarkably effective, calling not for strength or power, but for balance and posture, speed, clarity of mind and purpose; Now Tori is in a position to throw, concentrating his energies totally into completing the throwing action. The basic idea behind this move can be applied to numerous other techniques such as O-Goshi, Harai-Goshi, Tai-Otoshi and naturally works just as well for Hidari throws as Migi. It is best to practise this step very frequently, starting with your partner stepping twice as described, fairly slowly, and only gradually building up speed. After some practice, you should manage to perform the technique with your partner moving just one step, but the success does depend on the mastering, at least initially, of one's own smooth and controlled movement. For a right-hand Morote-Seoi-Nage a firm left-hand pull is crucial.

A good way of beginning to develop and feel this harmony is

to work blindfold. This has to be done with care – if both partners are working with their eyes shut they have to maintain an accurate awareness of their position on the mat, otherwise it will simply become dangerous. For this reason, it is recommended just to close the eyes rather than use an actual blindfold, so that one is not hindered in moments of sudden danger. It is surprising how rapidly the two partners become aware of their exact position on the mat, even after a fast and wide-ranging series of attacks. Bereft of vision, one begins to feel one's partner – where and how he moves, where are his strong points and where are his weak points. One's concentration is now so totally used in a different direction that one becomes less afraid of an attack and the whole practice becomes lighter and more fluent. Real harmony begins to manifest – it is surprising how often a throw such as De-Ashi-Barai seems to work the more we rely on feel rather than sight. This practice is enjoyed very much by children as well, but it is best to use some kind of blindfold so long as the instructor is watching carefully – children find it difficult to keep the eyes closed.

The principle of harmony applies equally to groundwork. Once again, an unnecessary amount of strength and brawn is often used in groundwork because, in the heat of the contest, all thoughts of harmony are lost. The tenth technique in Katame-no-Kata is a good example of the use of harmony over brawn.

The concept of harmony (like Circles, see page 49) applies to all aspects of Judo, whether in a complete throw or in one small detail. Kano insisted on harmony because, in typically practical Japanese manner, it was more efficient than cruder techniques. But there is another aspect not to be omitted even in a short chapter such as this. The beauty of Judo lies in the demonstration of harmony illustrated by a clean, effortless throw. No tough tug-around-the-mat concluding in a knock-down Koka can match the aesthetic satisfaction of a smooth and beautiful Kata-Guruma. Randori, Kata and even Shiai should always be performed in order to produce the best technique in the best possible way. The only importance of context is to demonstrate to what extent the participants have absorbed the fundamental principles of Judo and to put the participants in a position where they can draw the best out of themselves. A medal is a somewhat worthless object at the best of times, but a medal won by bad technique is unsatisfying at the very least, and at worst tarnishes the spirit of Judo itself.

Breaking the balance

Breaking your partner's balance is called Kuzushi and on its own is meaningless. The breaking of the balance with a throw can mean the difference between a good and a bad technique; when successfully applied, as part of a throw, Kuzushi then becomes Tsukuri.

Kuzushi

First, we will study the breaking of the balance without the throwing action. Standing in natural posture, we take a normal grip and our partner takes the same. By bending our knees slightly and maintaining the slight tension in our grip, we can bring our partner's balance forward sufficiently to control it momentarily. It is important not to make the action jerkily – this is to be a subtle method! That is all that is needed to control the balance in a forward direction.

Now let us try a rear method. Taking the same grip as before and exerting a slight pushing downward action with the wrists, we move our partner's balance rearward sufficiently to create the weakness we need to throw him. You will notice that at this stage neither of the Judoka are moving. It is best to approach the breaking of the balance step by step. This aspect of Judo is often one of the greatest weaknesses in Judoka of all grades, and it is a good idea to go back occasionally to the fundamental breaking of the balance action, practising while standing still. This method of subtle Kuzushi was extensively used by O-Tani Masuturo, who was known for the speed with which he could throw heavier opponents.

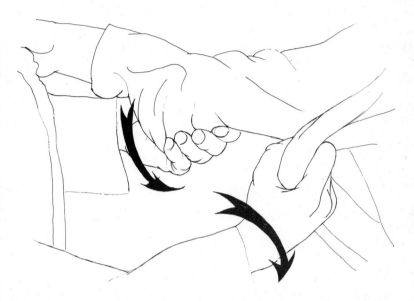

Just the twist of the wrists should be sufficient to break the balance, but the action is meaningless if the balance is not then controlled. And it won't happen with a partner in a stiff, solid, defensive posture – it has to be done 'on the move'.

Then progress to implementing the same action while moving. Keep the same grip and posture. Our partner takes a step back with his right foot and we break the balance forward as described. Return to the same posture. Now, as our partner takes a step forward with his right foot, we can break the balance rearward as previously described. Careful study and practice of these simple movements avoids the necessity to use unsubtle push and pull methods which may appear to be effective in the initial stages but which can later seriously hamper good Judo.

Tsukuri and timing

A common interpretation of Tsukuri is to pull one's partner off balance and, while holding him there, turn in for the throw. The aim, however, is for the control of breaking of the balance to be blended with the throwing action. This is one of the major reasons for the practice of Uchikomi: the breaking of the balance and the timing must be as much second nature as the execution of the throw itself.

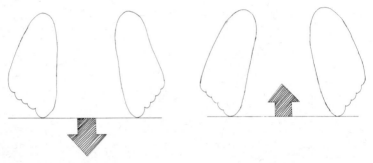

Kenshiro Abe's Kyu-Shin-Do school teaches that there are just two directions for breaking the balance, forwards or backwards, though if the line shifts, as when a step is taken, so do the directions in which the balance is to be broken.

In a sense, timing is synonymous with the Tsukuri action. As a guide to both timing and breaking the balance, let us imagine a line drawn across our partner's toes. Wherever our partner moves, the toe line is always there. Throws are always done at approximately right angles to this line, and not along it as breaking the balance is in two directions only, i.e. forward or backward. Many judo books discuss the breaking of the balance in other directions, such as right front or left rear. Kenshiro Abe taught that this is an unnecessary complication, even with a throw such as Okuri-Ashi-Barai which is often taught with the premise that the balance is broken sideways. The principle of breaking the balance backwards or forwards holds true for

Okuri-Ashi-Barai as well. You break the balance with a wrist action towards you, timing the action when your partner moves one foot towards the other. Another example of timing, using Morote-Seoi-Nage, could be when your partner steps back on his right foot. As he steps back, we use that same wrist action to break his balance, at the same time turning in for the throw.

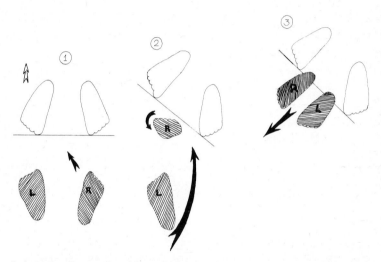

It is important to be able to make the most of every opportunity your opponent offers, rather than to wait until he makes a very bad mistake, or until you can 'set him up'. Theoretically, every time your opponent steps, he is putting himself at risk and can be taken advantage of, as here.

These are just two examples, but the same principles should be applied to all throws, for all throws require the correct timing, and all throws need control, however slight, of a partner's balance. Correct, subtle Tsukuri is not easy to master, but eventually frequently proves a dominant factor in contests.

Many Judoka, particularly those concentrating on competitive work of national or international standing, feel that within the stiffer conditions of contest, only a strong, powerful Kuzushi really works, and Uchikomi is practised using a considerable pull to bring one's partner on to the toes. This is not, of course, in accord with Jigoro Kano's traditional principle of 'Maximum Efficiency with Minimum Effort', though this is not in itself sufficient to discard the power-Kuzushi: tradition must always be proven to work in modern conditions or the tradition becomes merely sterile ritual. Certainly, the contest Judoka has to contend with people who stand deep in Jigotai or defensive posture and who are unusually strong due to severe weight-training programmes and simply do not react in a light and sensitive manner.

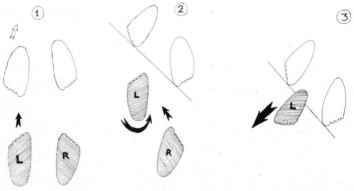

Another example of using the principle of Tsukuri to its full advantage. Uke steps back with his right foot. Tori advances his left foot, aiming to place it just in front of Uke's right foot – but before Uke's right foot has finally come to rest. With correct Kuzushi (which here really means just preventing Uke's shoulders from regaining good posture) Tori can pivot in on that placed left foot for the Migi-Harai-Goshi

But the reliance on a 'power type' Kuzushi is dependent upon highly developed physique and is not applicable to Judoka without it! Taken to its logical conclusion, therefore, this approach could drive out the lighter men or women, for although contests may be divided into weight categories, those of lighter physique still have to contend with and survive rough actions in normal club practice. And in those conditions, with the 'power'-

Kuzushi dominating the practice, the little man finds even ordinary progress difficult.

One crucial aspect of Kuzushi is, in fact, rarely mentioned in Dojos, and is only discovered by Judoka through hard but thoughtful work. The immensely strong Judoka relies on pulling his partner towards and on top of him as he approaches for a throw. The lighter and more skilful Judoka has, however, an alternative – he can break the balance with a relatively small action while at the same time using the 'pull' to slide his body under his partner's. A good example of this can be seen in Morote Seoi-Otoshi. A correct Kuzushi will bring Uke on to his

By relying on power and strength, Tori inevitably pays less attention to speed and timing. For a small Judoka, such reliance on strength is pointless, but even the bigger Judoka will always meet someone who is bigger and stronger – or faster and more agile. The temptation, however, to turn exclusively to the weights room rather than the Tatami after a few 'heavy' contests, is very great

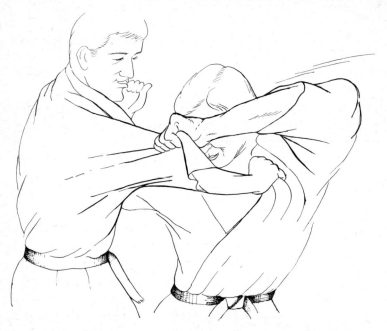

An efficient left-hand pull is one of the most crucial aspects of right-handed hip and shoulder techniques: too powerful and too jerky, and your partner has resisted or side-stepped; too weak and your partner's balance remains unbroken. Yet this basic aspect of standing techniques often fails to be mastered until well after 1st Dan. The left-hand pull should be made with the feeling of the point of the elbow leading the movement, though in fact the movement should start from the right hip. The hand twists at the wrist from a palm-up to a palm down motion as the elbow leads upwards so that the partner's upper sleeve should be around the area of your face – not somewhere around your midriff. If you get to this situation you know you have control and can continue without fear of being countered. One tip: When practising, having effected the pull, test the left bicep. If it is clenched and strained, the action is not coming from the hips; if it is relaxed, it is correct. Incidentally, the theory is: the twisting action breaks the balance, the pull controls the balance (see page 41)

toes, but Tori may not be deep enough in position to bring off the throw. However, if Tori combines his Kuzushi action with a slide which takes him deeper into the position for the throw he will find himself lower and in a more advantageous and stronger posture. This is a simple action to feel but difficult to describe. Diligent practice will improve a whole series of hip techniques, and even other throws such as Tomoe-Nage and Sasae-Tsuri-Komi-Goshi where the same feeling of drawing your partner above you as you slide yourself slightly underneath exists. The basic action is beautifully illustrated in the last technique of Itsutsu-no-Kata, except that there it is done in a form of Yoko-Wakare with the Judoka not touching.

However, before the 'slide' can be put into effect, an opening has to be created to allow the entry, and it is at this point that it is worthwhile going back to basic principles. It is very difficult for a small man to throw a big man who is stationary and stiff. The small man's great asset is speed, which he can use to loosen the big man and make him step. It is here that the combinations really come into their own. Instead of thinking of a huge Kuzushi to preface the one big throw, think of the best position for your partner to be in for you to make a successful attack, and then consider how to invite them into that position.

There is an infinite number of possible combinations which can be developed towards this end, but one simple example is De-Ashi-Barai into Seoi-Otoshi. Tori attacks Uke's left foot with a De-Ashi-Barai really aiming for that technique. If Uke sees it coming, he will often react by just sliding his foot back, or lifting it over the attack. Tori then continues the sweeping action, but at the same time twists into the Seoi-Otoshi position, making just a slight Kuzushi action. Even a big man is, at this point, so off-balance that the normal subtle Kuzushi action is all that is necessary to bring him well on to his toes, enabling the throw to be completed without undue strength or effort. This kind of attack doesn't come easily. Much more practise is needed to develop a smooth, fluid action in the first De-Ashi-Barai attack and the change into Seoi-Otoshi, than a 'power'-Kuzushi.

What's more, everything has to be right – not just the foot movements of the first and second attacks, but the arm movements too, especially the high left-hand pull of the Seoi-Otoshi (see page 46).

The first time this works in Randori or Shiai will be a real eye-opener – Uke goes so easily, so lightly and so fast, that one is tempted to believe that he has jumped for you – which, in a way, he has. And aesthetically, a 'power'-Kuzushi is simply not in the same league.

There is also another method of breaking the balance that is worth practising, upon which Kenshiro Abe placed great importance.

Reverse Principle

You are facing your partner holding in normal grip and standing in normal posture. You make the hand/wrist action towards you, as if you were going to throw in that direction. Then, as

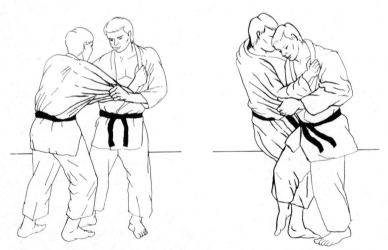

Tori pulls Uke with a short, sharp movement towards him. Uke invariably then reacts by pulling back, enabling Tori to move in for the O-Soto-Gari. This is Reverse Principle

your partner resists this movement by pulling back, you use Tsukuri in a rear throw, using, for example, O-Soto-Gari.

The reverse principle is very effective, but does require a high technical standard in order to make the best use of it. Your actions must in the first instance be of short movement in order to get the desired reaction, and in the second part blend smoothly into the complete Tsukuri in whatever throw you choose. Naturally, this applies equally for a forward throw, involving a short Kuzushi to the rear before the forward Tsukuri.

Circles

Judo is based on the circle. In fact, it is no exaggeration to say that the circle is present in virtually all Judo techniques, whether

Judo is based on the circle

in just the hand action of the Kuzushi or the whole body movement during Kake, the throw in its entirety, or, to go even further, in the whole body movements of two practising Judoka. Each separate movement of the limbs involves a circular movement, or part of a circle. Closing the fingers as you take a grip, rotating the wrist as you apply a strangle, rotating the body as you turn in for a throw – the circle is always there. Watch someone's hand action as they throw, for example, in Morote-Seoi-Nage: the Tsukuri and Kake, if correctly controlled are of a circular motion.

Yet often on the mat it is obvious that many Judokas are unaware of this natural, circular use of the body, and their actions more closely resemble dragdowns, shoves or kicks.

An obvious, but nevertheless beautiful, example of the circular movement is Kata-Guruma. During the throwing action, Kake, Uke's balance is transferred over Tori's back and Uke describes a perfect circle. It is significant that Kata Guruma is often a small-man's throw (though everyone should be able to get low enough for it) involving little strength but a lot of technique.

Circular movement actually exists in all throws (and break-falls). Often, when techniques fail, it is because Tori has tried to short-cut a circle, creating a sharp angle. An oft-quoted, but nevertheless important example is the left-hand pull in a Migi Tai-Otoshi. Unless Tori describes quite a large circle with his left-hand pull, he draws Uke directly onto him, making the throw impossible. That left-hand circle is a crucially important factor in many other throws.

The importance Jigoro Kano placed on the principle of the circle can be demonstrated by the Kata that he developed, Itsutsu-no-Kata, the Kata of the Five Principles. This is the form which symbolizes circular movement in nature.

We have already stated that circular movements are important in all throws, and we must add that they are important in avoiding and countering actions. Our partner turns in for his throw straight towards us, and we must avoid in one of several ways:

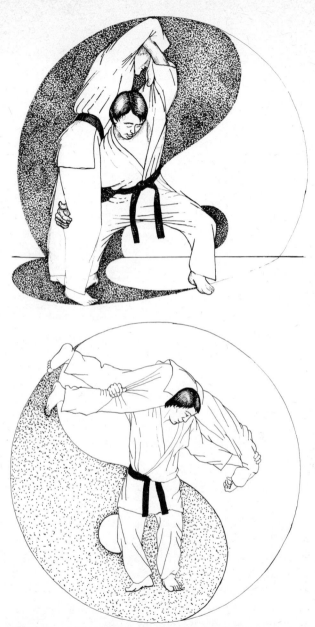

The action of Kata-Guruma should describe a perfect circle, smooth, unruffled and elegant, giving little indication of the technical complexities involved; and at the centre of the circle – Hara

51

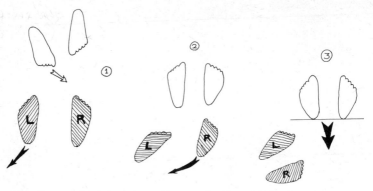

Avoiding to the left. When Uke attacks with a right-handed technique, it is possible to avoid by moving to the left, and taking Uke down to the ground. This is effective when Uke's attack is weakened by bad posture – particularly when he is bending backwards. Using this at the wrong time – when Uke's posture is very good – leaves you (Tori) very vulnerable to a spectacular throw

1 To the left.
2 To the right.
3 Over the top in the direction of the throw.
4 Lower our weight, maintaining the same position.
5 Miscellaneous.
When avoiding to the left or right, do not cross your legs.

Methods 1 and 2 take you out of danger, upsets your partner's balance momentarily, and places you in an ideal position for a counter-throw.

Method 3 is applicable when you are unable to use (or choose not to use) Methods 1 and 2. Let us say that your partner turns in for Morote-Seoi-Nage. Both your hands must keep their grip on your partner's jacket, and you use this grip to control your partner's throwing move, enabling you to land on the Tatami on your side in front of your partner and finish with Yoko-Guruma. The use of Sumi-Gaeshi as a counter to Ippon-Seoi-Nage is a similar example. The use of Sumi-Gaeshi is not, however, generally applicable as a counter to Harai-Goshi or Hane-Goshi as one can be caught in mid-air, countered ourselves by the Harai or Hane-Goshi transformed into Uchi-Mata. But Sumi-Gaeshi is a viable counter to Morote-Seoi-Nage, or even O-Goshi, and demonstrates both principles of circular movement and positive action.

In Method 4 you bend your knees, not your body, so that you are under your partner's attack and can use a counter-throw such as Utsuri-Goshi or Tani-Otoshi. The first three methods mean that you make a small circular action to avoid your partner's attack, leaving you in a good position to counter-attack. The fourth method is needed when you are perhaps not quick enough to use Methods 1 or 2 or not sufficiently skilful in the use of sacrifice throws (Sutemi-Waza).

But as often as not, the same throw that your partner attacks with can be used as a counter, provided you avoid his move first. Examples of these can be grouped under Method 5 which I call Miscellaneous because they are really individual reactions to certain attacks. For instance, if attacked by O-Soto-Gari, you do not avoid, but as your partner makes contact, you pull down on his right sleeve, an action which gives you momentary control of

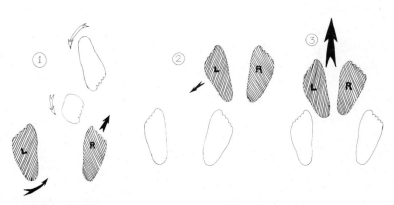

Avoiding to the right. Uke attacks with Morote-Seoi-Nage. Tori avoids to his right and places himself in position for a left-handed technique – Tai-Otoshi, Seoi-Otoshi, O-Goshi – the choice is wide

Rather than avoiding Morote-Seoi-Nage by resisting, go with the throw, in a controlled move over your opponent's hip. He thinks he has you and injects extra effort which helps to carry you over into Sumi-Gaeshi. It is a technique demonstrating all the principles of yielding in Judo, but needs real control to prevent a slight misjudgment which leads to a spectacular throw

his balance. You can now throw him in O-Soto-Gari. Another example of miscellaneous attacks can be found in one of the most popular of throws, Uchi-Mata. As your partner attacks, bring your left leg behind you and then step forward on your right; control your partner's balance and counter with Te-Waza, i.e. Uki-Otoshi or Sukui-Nage. The two examples given here should be sufficient to provoke other ideas and possibilities. The most important point is that in all aspects, your attitude must be positive and your actions circular.

In combination techniques, an understanding of circular movement is essential for the continuation of your attacking actions. Mr Kenshiro Abe always taught that from each separate technique should stem three more. See this idea as the branches of a tree, from each branch coming three other branches.

Your partner can often counter a single attack, but will have difficulty if you have prepared for this by applying a combination technique. He may avoid the second technique of the combination, but will most certainly have trouble if you apply a third. Each of your actions of the combination is triggered off by your partner's reaction to your move. For example, we attack with De-Ashi Barai to our partner's right leg; he then takes a step back to avoid this and we continue into Ouchi-Gari to our partner's left leg; he avoids by lifting his leg clear, and we continue into a Migi Tai-Otoshi. The action of changing from one technique to another must be smooth, circular and fast, just as the throw involves fast, circular movements.

Just as all circles have a centre, so all throws must have a centre. The centre of the human body is roughly two inches below the navel, the Tanden (see page 32). The execution of a throw involves Tori in taking control of Uke's balance and, in hip throws at least, makes Tori's Tanden the central pivot point of the larger circle described by Uke when he is thrown. That is why awareness of the Tanden and awareness of the circle are crucial in good Judo, and in all the martial arts.

Groundwork

Posture, and the principles of harmony and the circle apply as much to groundwork (Katamewaza) as to throwing techniques (Nage-Waza). Groundwork should not involve a clash of strength and, once again, there is no reason at all why the larger, stronger man should dominate. The alert Judoka must be able to take what comes, and be prepared to change from one technique to another in a fluid, positive motion.

Groundwork techniques can be divided into three groups:

1 When you are on top of your partner as in a hold-down.
2 When you are underneath your partner.
3 When you are in an equal position to your partner.

This is to be regarded only as a key to the study of ground-work as there can also be added a fourth section for miscellaneous techniques which do not fit into the previous three. If we look at the value of hold-downs (Osae-komi-Waza) we find that they fit only the first category, whereas if we look at armlocks and chokes/strangles, we find they fit any group – they can be applied whether we are underneath, on top or level with an opponent. It is strange, therefore, that a greater emphasis is generally placed on hold-downs, whereas they can only be used in one-third of our groundwork. In fact, strangles and chokes can be a great equalizer for the lighter Judoka and should be studied and practised with the same regularity as standing techniques.

In chokes we prevent our partner from breathing fully, and a look at the reason for this explains why the lighter or weaker person can benefit from a study of these techniques. There is no muscle structure in the front of a person's throat so even a comparatively weak person, when positioned well, can make an effective technique on a stronger person. Even the strong muscle grouping in the sides of the neck can be used against a stronger opponent by pressing those muscles against the carotid artery and the jugular vein – in other words by applying a strangle. The muscle structure is there in the neck to control the head's movement, not as a protection for the arteries and veins; and in Judo, we make the most of a weakness.

Most armlocks are applied when the arm is straight as in Ude-Kujiki-Juji-Gatame or bent at the elbow as in Ude-Garami, but students are always instructed to fake an armlock attack in order to use a choke, or vice versa.

If the opportunity arises to use a hold-down, then do so, but always be aware of the possibility of changing to an armlock or strangle – especially if your partner is escaping from the hold. Do not try to maintain a hold-down position if your partner is escaping, but have the flexibility of mind and fluency of technique to change to another form of attack.

One example is a swift change from a weak Kesa-Gatame to a

form of Ude-Kujiki-Juji-Gatame, turning Uke's escaping move to Tori's advantage. Uke is escaping from a Migi-Kesa-Gatame by pulling away with his right hand and turning to the left. Tori maintains a firm control over Uke's forearm or wrist under his own left arm and places his left hand on Uke's right elbow. Tori's left leg is now swiftly brought across Uke's throat and the armlock is applied with pressure from the hips (see plates 14a and b).

Another simple but effective technique is the disguised approach to a choke such as when Tori is applying Migi-Yoko-Shiho-Gatame and it appears that Uke is escaping by turning away from Tori. Tori brings his right arm away from between the legs and discreetly slides it under his body and takes a grip (fingers inside) of Uke's left-side lapel, high up around the neck. Tori now raises his hips and, with the right leg shooting through, twisting the body, the right forearm applies pressure to Uke's neck. The effectiveness of the technique depends on:

1 The craftiness of the initial approach;
2 That the whole of Tori's body is concentrated into the choke;
3 And that Tori's hands should, as with most strangles and chokes, be as close together as possible.

Techniques such as these may not work at the beginning because some small element of detail is missing, and instant success must not be expected. But perseverance will result in a far greater security of technique – especially when moving around on the ground.

Kuzushi and Tsukuri are also crucial in groundwork, and again subtlety rather than strength should be nurtured. Reverse Principle too can be successfully applied, especially when allied to a firm kneeling posture (with the toes of the kneeling leg always curled under for extra control).

Times of attack

It is interesting to note that in Kendo (the Way of the Sword) there are five optimum times to attack:

1 A moment of distraction (such as blinking, or an outside disturbance or thought).
2 Immediately prior to the beginning of any action of your partner.
3 As the mind is involved in the finish of the action.
4 As the mind is involved in the beginning of the action.
5 As the mind relaxes just after the completion of the action.

It is not enough just to memorize these times: one has to practise them. Very often, in Randori or Shiai, we see or feel an opportunity to attack, but our physical response to the thought is too slow. However, by practise, we can shorten the time between thought and action. Move around lightly with a partner and make arbitrary decisions when to move in. At the beginning, it doesn't matter so much whether the timing is right or not. Just think, 'Attack', and see how long it takes your body to respond. After a while, the period will shorten considerably. Of course, more often than not, mental and physical activity during a Randori or Contest is far too fast for a conceptual approach like this – the Judoka must develop a kind of trained instinct. Nevertheless, this sort of practice does improve the command we have over our own bodies and we learn not only to react more quickly, but create actions in the first place. There is no point in drawing a partner into a vulnerable position if at the crucial time our physical actions fall seriously short of the demands made by our mental processes – in other words, if we see the opportunity but are too slow to take advantage of it.

There are various ways of building up fluency of attack outside the standard Randori, which often has a strongly competitive atmosphere which inhibits the smooth flow of movement. One way is for one partner to be Uke and practise avoiding, being light and swift in his movements, while Tori

pours in a constant stream of attacks, left, right, forward, backward, combinations, sacrifice techniques, etc. Then Tori and
Uke switch roles. This can be tiring but immensely valuable
practice for both in order to build up a feeling for continuous,
purposeful attacks.

Another method is alternating throws for two minutes. One
throws, the other gets up quickly, takes hold and, as his partner
moves, throws. The actions should be fast and almost instinctive
– try not to decide which throw to execute as you get up, but let
the movement of your partner dictate your throw. Uke should
not be obstructive, but at the same time not too co-operative.
Masutaro O-Tani once wrote:

> Many people have started with me doing my type of very
> fast Judo, but when they want to train in contest technique,
> start power training. They cannot see it, but I can see how
> their speed drops.
>
> Over and again I say you must have speed and timing.
> Some people are very fast, but attack at the wrong time,
> that is, when your opponent is standing still. Because of
> attacking at this wrong time you will be counter thrown. I
> now teach Uchi-Komi stepping in and out, so that you may
> get used to attacking when your opponent moves.
>
> When I was studying under Yukio Tani, I thought I was
> getting on very well, but he would come up behind me,
> shake my shoulders without saying a word, and walk
> away. I knew very well he meant my shoulders were too
> stiff to do good Judo. (*Judoka*, vol. VII, no 2)

Grips

Since its inception, Judo has been based on one great assump-
tion, that the two Judoka working together take normal grips at
the beginning of a contest. However, some Judoka prefer to
fight for grips hoping to gain some small advantage – whether

The practice of Judo

psychological or tactical; it is a habit particularly noticeable when Judo is practised with a medal mentality.

Almost always, the best approach is to allow the opponent to take whatever grip he wants and then to settle down to Judo, but beware of the sudden attack from the one-handed grip. The best way of remaining unaffected by obstructive grips is to practise all techniques from a variety of grips, Migi and Hidari. The Judoka, however, must be prepared to take a grip less suited to his technique, and gradually, subtly, obtain a more favoured grip as the contest continues.

Of course, obstructive grips are only one side of the common grips problem. The other is the stiff, strong arm grip, but there are a variety of ways to combat it. Taking Moroto-Seoi-Nage as an example, let us look first at the stiff right arm and then the stiff left.

If Uke's right arm is driving into Tori's chest, Tori must incorporate a 'snap action' into the turn-in (for the Migi Moroto-Seoi-Nage) in order to dislodge the right arm and turn the stiffness to his own advantage. Note that it is not enough just to snap-turn; Tori's left-hand pull must, at the same time, be high and sharp (see page 46).

Now, the left arm. If Uke's left arm is gripping Tori's right sleeve in a stiff manner, Tori feints with a move of his right elbow slightly upwards and to the right, and then again, with a sudden snap-action, brings it into the conventional Migi-Morote position. It is immaterial whether Uke holds on or lets go. If Uke is stiff and unyielding in both arms, then both snap-actions have to be implemented simultaneously. This dual technique requires much work to be effective, but it will work. The basic dual snap-action is also effective with O-Goshi, Harai-Goshi and many similar techniques.

The main principle underlying the grips problem is never to sacrifice good posture which would prevent you from throwing or countering efficiently or well.

60

Thinking through contests

It is not enough to practise hard and enter contests with a trained body and a quiet mind. It has often been said that Judo is a bit like chess, and it is necessary to think through contests and prepare where possible. If we know we are going to face a much larger or a much smaller person than ourselves, then some techniques can immediately be put to one side, or at least into a 'reserve' bank. For instance, if a much larger man is contesting with a smaller man, then throws such as Morote-Seoi-Nage or Kata-Guruma or Seoi-Otoshi would generally be unsuitable for the former and Harai-Goshi and O-Guruma unsuitable for the latter. It may be helpful, also, to have a sketchy blueprint for the five-minute contest. Obviously, one must not adhere rigidly to a plan, but it can help to map out different areas of attack if bereft of inspiration in the heat of the moment. Of course, if two or three attempts of a favourite technique have failed, there is no point in hammering away at it. One can make a false attack and see what it is in our opponent's reaction that prevents the technique from succeeding, and then attempt a disguised attack in the light of that knowledge. But we have to be able to vary our mental approach, from the prepared to the instinctive.

It is also important, throughout our Judo, and especially in contests, not to allow distractions to interfere. Whether doing Randori or Shiai, the concentration on the work in hand must be total – while retaining an awareness of other people on the mat and one's position within the mat area.

Beginner's mind

Shoshin means 'original mind' or 'beginner's mind' and incorporates the best qualities in a beginner which, only too often, the Judoka loses as his training progresses. Shoshin involves a single-mindedness and concentration, a certain amount of innocence and openness and a simplicity of approach. The ideas and movements of Judo appear so complex and so varied that the whole attention of the beginner is absorbed. He doesn't think about what happened during the day or what he is going to do tomorrow; or that if he moves in for an Ogoshi in the manner suggested by his Sensei his partner might avoid and counter in this or that manner. His approach is often so simple that it works, even though he is actually lacking in technique.

But after he has been training for some time and becomes more familiar with basic techniques, he allows his concentration to slip and begins to consider the ifs and buts of suggested techniques. This is natural and necessary, but unfortunately, other unnecessary thoughts also begin to permeate his practice: self-doubt, anxiety, anger towards himself, aggression towards others, frustration and embarrassment. All these emotions inhibit clear, clean Judo, yet so often they are exhibited on the mat: more often than not the most difficult opponent is one's own mind.

It is important to maintain a balanced view of oneself, not kicking oneself for an unsuccessful technique, and not leaping in the air with joy after a successful technique, but just acknowledging both for what they are – and learning from both. As any experienced Judoka knows, the best techniques appear to happen in spite of oneself, in a curious limbo outside time, outside effort, outside perception: neither the thrower nor the person thrown remembers very much afterwards other than one person landing squarely on his back. Excessive self-congratulation by Tori implies excessive negative self-criticism by Uke. Neither attitudes should have any place in Judo.

Sometimes it happens that the naive beginner moves in for a technique and by the sheer effrontery of his simplicity, it works without effort. The beginner himself is not surprised because that is what he thought he was working towards. All the other watching Kyu grades are astounded – they could probably list a dozen reasons why that technique should not have worked. It can take many years for the Judoka to let go of all these inhibiting emotions and thoughts, and return to the simplicity of the beginner – although now armed with clarity and technique. Sadly, not many last the course. How much better then to discard these complicating factors immediately they arise in oneself. Sometimes these factors remain on a mental level, but often they translate themselves into physical actions. A common example is with Morote-Seoi-Nage and numerous other hip and shoulder techniques. After a few attempts have failed, Judoka become impatient and frustrated and decided that what they need is more momentum, and therefore step back with the right leg in order to swing in. But what this effectively does is warn your partner that you are about to attempt a right-hand technique and gives him ample time to avoid or counter. This is one of the numerous 'improvements' made by Judoka travelling through the Kyu grades which are later discarded. The journey is generally faster and lighter without them.

Another important attribute of the beginner is enthusiasm. There is a lot of repetition in Judo which can become tedious unless a bright, enquiring and above all enthusiastic approach is maintained. If you are finding a dullness entering your practice, it is a good idea to change the people with whom you practise, perhaps just for a short while. Visit a beginner's class occasionally, help out at a children's class, and as a last resort, stop practising for a week or two.

Open mind

It is crucial not to erect mental barriers when practising – more often than not the most formidable opponent one meets on the mat is oneself. People say: 'I will never throw him, look at his size, look at his grade.' Another favourite is: 'He is an expert at Uchi-Mata, I must watch that.' As soon as you comment on your opponent's size or ability, you are presupposing that size or grade is of such importance that you will lose. You can throw a bigger person in contest if you are technically on form, both physically and mentally. A primary object of Judo is to train to a standard where your opponent is of secondary importance; he is there solely as an obstacle to be overcome, using your Judo ability at its best. That is a general point. More specifically, if you watch out for one technique, you will probably be thrown in something you were not watching for.

Yoyu in this context is best translated as 'Open Mind'. If you have an open mind in contest or practice, you are able to take whatever comes in your stride. You will be able to react more quickly and your movements will be more positive and faster. An open mind does not mean that you stop thinking. We all tend to have pre-arranged ideas and preferences for techniques. We enter contests looking for the moment when we can set up our opponent for our favourite throw, and in the process miss numerous other equally valid opportunities. Strategy and plans do have a place in Judo, but the experienced Judoka must be ready to discard or change those plans instantly without loss of mental equilibrium. Flexibility of mind is of the utmost importance.

Aggression

Aggression does not have a valid place in Judo, in spite of the fact that in the context of Judo as a sport, a show of aggression can mean the difference between victory or defeat. On the other hand, limp techniques are meaningless. The word determination is preferable.

In Randori or contest, the Judoka should aim for a pure attacking spirit, a commitment to the contest and to the techniques attempted which will admit no other thoughts, thoughts of failure, or overconfidence.

The word aggression involves anger, a win-at-any-cost attitude which is inimical to the true spirit of Judo. There must, however, be a one hundred per cent sense of commitment and determination.

We are human, however, and there will be many occasions

when we are not one hundred per cent fit physically or mentally ourselves, yet we have agreed to take part in a contest or Randori. What we should not do is 'psyche' ourselves up in an attempt to reach an artificial peak, but hone ourselves down to a sharp point. Trevor Leggett has described this attitude in an appropriately poetic image: if we have only thirty per cent of our peak one hundred per cent state to give to a contest or a Randori, that thirty per cent should be as effective as an arrow-head.

In any case, each throw should be executed like a whip-crack.

4 Kata

Dr Jigoro Kano regarded Kata as 'the essence of Judo'. In this he was continuing the ancient Ju-Jitsu tradition which distilled the numerous techniques and counters into a pre-arranged sequence of moves which combined both the practical methods of defence and the aesthetic qualities of the techniques. As such, Kata is enormously rewarding to all Judoka, whether junior or senior, contest men or teachers.

Often, contest Judoka regard Kata as an unnecessary distraction from valuable Randori time, beneficial only to teachers unable to contest. This is a serious misunderstanding. The Katas were formed for use as a living record of the insights of past masters, to serve as a kind of moving text-book. The only real way to learn Judo techniques is to watch, listen and practise. Initially, the Judoka learns individual techniques, a bit like, in language terms, learning a stilted list of unconnected vocabulary. But when a Judoka learns a Kata, which is at first deceptively difficult, he is acquiring a basic, moving grammar. By carefully learning the Kata in the first place, and then maintaining it by practising it at least twice or more a week, the movements become second nature. As soon as Uke pushes in attack, Tori moves in fluid response, rather than responding with a sense of jerky surprise, as only too often happens in Randori. Obvious, but worth stating, the particular techniques which have been woven into Kata have been chosen because they have been proved to work in contest. They are not empty theory, but the distillation of experience. Thus the contest Judoka stands to gain substantially by diligent practice of Kata.

It may help to outline various specific areas of benefit gained by practising Kata.

The practice of Kata involves paying attention to precision on a number of levels. The Judoka slowly becomes aware of the balance or imbalance of his partner, of his feet and body position, of his direction and impetus at all points of the throw. The same detailed awareness of precision applies to himself – if the technique is not working, if, for instance, Uke does not land on the line of Kata, some slight aspect of his own technique must be wrong. It is frequently only the severe constraints of Kata that encourage the average Judoka to work and correct the most minute detail. This inevitably feeds and improves all his other Judo.

The discipline and even the elusiveness of Kata demands that two people work in very close harmony. This, in itself, can be most illuminating. Two partners working together over a period of time learn to respect the strengths of each other and acknowledge their weaknesses in a non-competitive, open and mutually beneficial manner, overcoming pride, prejudice and petty irritations. This acts as a marvellous blueprint for normal social intercourse.

There are times in every Judoka's life when for no apparent reason one's technique seems to disintegrate. We may not have changed our practice routine, or our diligence, but everything seems to have fallen apart – timing, speed, precision – so that we have difficulty in throwing even much lower grades. This can be a painful and frustrating time, both physically and psychologically, and it is at this time that the strength of Kata is invaluable. By submitting ourselves, as it were, to an established, external pattern, we can keep our Judo alive and receptive and allow our normal standard to reassert itself in its own time.

Finally, Kata demonstrates in a satisfying and ever challenging manner, the aesthetic depth of Judo. Often the Judoka is too involved in the heat of contest or Randori, or the earnestness of Uchikomi, to appreciate the beauty and subtlety of the art he practises. A superb performance of a Kata is an extraordinarily uplifting experience, one that permeates the participants for long after the Kata has finished. It sometimes happens that a Judoka may perform a technique well in Randori, starting and finishing with a creditable posture, but as soon as he bows off to his partner and walks to another part of the Tatami, his alertness and calm disappears. But in Nage-no-Kata, for example, he learns to bear himself well throughout the demonstration, between the techniques themselves. Every hand and foot movement must be done with mindfullness: not like a zombie, but purposefully and with direction. In that sense, the Katas present an ideal of human activity and behaviour, one worth remembering when walking down the street, or in everyday life. It is worth noting that in Nage-no-Kata, for instance, Tori always yields twice before throwing Uke unless it is a serious attack such as a blow, or when already entwined as in Uke Waza. It is details such as these which make the Katas an ever-fascinating study whatever one's stage of Judo. It could be said that the standard of one's Kata reflects one's true understanding of Judo in all its aspects.

General points

It is important not to leave the preparation of Kata to a few days before the grading in the hope that the techniques can be picked up quickly. A Kata is to be performed as one entire event, not as a compilation of separate techniques. It is crucial, therefore, to pay as much attention right from the beginning to the links in between the techniques as the techniques themselves. The flow and the grace of Kata only comes with time and practice. If you cobble a Kata together in a hurry, it will look like it, no matter how good your contest techniques, because the spirit of the Kata will not have been absorbed.

At demonstrations or Kata competitions, the following points must be noted: Uke should always be the taller of the two, and Tori the higher grade; if one of the two is a woman, she must always be Tori and never Uke. Particular attention must be paid to Judogi which should be clean and the right size, and which should not be covered with badges which, if they are worn, should be limited to one or two and placed on the lower left flap below the belt.

Nage-no-Kata

This Kata has fifteen throws which are practised both left and right, giving a good balance of technique. Very few people learn throws both ways in normal practice, even though contest demands that top Judoka should be able to take advantage of every opportunity given.

The beginner to this Kata should start by learning the five main divisions: Te-Waza (hand and shoulder techniques); Koshi-Waza (hip and loin techniques); Ashi-Waza (leg and foot techniques); Ma-Sutemi-Waza (rear sacrifices); and Yoko-Sutemi-Waza (side sacrifices).

Each of these divisions has three throws, but the moves should not be learned in isolation. In linking them together, care must be taken to practise the required formal steps in between the techniques: where Uke returns to his starting point for the next throw, and turns to face Tori, and so on.

When starting the Kata, particularly at demonstrations or Kata competitions, Uke and Tori rei (bow) first to Joseki (the judges or higher grades) and then to each other. At the start of each set, both must take a small left-right step to open the feet after the rei. In the techniques where Uke is attacking Tori in Yoko-Uchi (side head blow) there should be sufficient space between the two for Uke to take two forward steps when attacking. It is poor technique by Uke to take one step back and then one forward.

Each of the techniques of Nage-no-Kata has its own speed and timing and 'feel'. The speed should vary with the technique – Kata Guruma should be performed more slowly than Okuri Ashi Barai, for instance, but the participants themselves have to decide optimum speed.

Some of the throws, such as Yoko Guruma, Uki Waza or Yoko Gake, are not generally practised in contest nowadays, but they are still useful techniques. In fact, many Judoka would never have the chance to learn such a wide variety of techniques were it not for the Katas.

It is fairly common for practitioners of other martial arts to speak about Judo in derogatory terms, remarking that Judo is useless for self-defence. Even a cursory glance at Nage-no-Kata contradicts this: Kata-Seoi-Nage, Uke Goshi, Ura Nage, Yoko Guruma and others are all very effective in self-defence situations, if performed well.

Katame-no-Kata

This is the Kata which demonstrates groundwork techniques and, again, there are fifteen in all, but this time divided into three categories: Osae-Waza (hold-downs), Shime-Waza (strangles); and Kansetsu-Waza (armlocks).

The choice of hold-down techniques has been carefully decided to demonstrate various ways of controlling and immobilizing a partner, and are not meant as submission techniques. These are for Judo contest only, and not for self-defence. When being held, Uke should start to struggle when Tori, having established the hold, makes a 'tightening up' action.

Next come the chokes and strangleholds which are demonstrations of submission techniques, and finally the armlocks and the leglock to finish the Kata. It may appear strange to have a leglock in the demonstration when it is not allowed in contest, but it should be remembered that this was at one time a permissible technique, and one that was very effective too.

Between each set, Uke and Tori return to kneeling position and of course begin and end the Kata with a full kneeling rei. It is not necessary to use the high kneeling posture with the right leg moved out to the side each time as this is only relevant when wearing Hakama, not normal Judogi. The whole of this Kata

1 A formal Japanese dinner held to welcome Dr Jigoro Kano, the founder of Kodokan Judo, paying his second visit to Britain. Dr Kano sits under the picture of Mount Fuji. To his right, at the end of the top table, sits Mr Kotani, now 9th Dan, who spent some months at the Budokwai as a full-time instructor. On the right of the picture, at the top of the long table, is E. J. Harrison, Gunji Koizumi, an unknown Judoka, and Marcus Kaye

2   Visitors and members of the Budokwai in the late 1920s. Sitting cross-legged in the centre is Yukio Tani. On his left is Ozawa and C. Cawkell. Seated in chairs, from left to right, are Gunji Koizumi, founder of the Budokwai, E. J. Harrison, one of the first Britons ever to learn Judo in Japan (he studied in the first decade of this century); also seated (with spotted bow-tie), Dr Shepherd. Standing, on the extreme right of the picture, Mr Frank Hammond

3   Yukio Tani (1881–1950) at his peak as a Judo/Ju-Jitsu exponent,
unbeaten by any wrestler of any Western style in hundreds of challenge
contests in Britain's music halls

4   Leg-locks used to be part of Judo in the very early days – here Yukio
Tani, in a photograph taken from his book *The Game of Ju-Jitsu* written with
Taro Miyake, demonstrates a standing leg-lock using pressure against the
base of the calf, a very tender spot

5 Gunji Koizumi (1885–1965), father of European Judo and founder of the Budokwai, who was also an expert in Chinese lacquer

6   Gunji Koizumi demonstrating Yama-Arashi. Notice how the controlled circular left-hand action, in conjunction with the right-hand action, has brought Uke well on to his toes

7   Kenshiro Abe (b. 1916), 8th Dan, Judo, but also highly skilled in Kendo and Aikido, standing in a London Dojo. Behind him, a poster advertising one of the big demonstrations of Judo, Karate, Kendo and Aikido run by Mr Abe during the early 1960s attended by leading exponents such as H. Michigami, the prominent Judoka who did so much to develop Judo in France

8   Kenshiro Abe, founder of the British Judo Council, teaching Kyu-Shin-Judo in a Dojo along the South Coast, on one of the hundreds of courses he conducted which were always very popular

9   Masutaro Otani (1898–1977), 8th Dan, one of the most well-known
Judoka in Britain and also former President of the British Judo Council

10   Masutaro Otani teaches his method of Tai-Otoshi at a class with the
author, Alan Fromm

11 Masutaro Otani, who led the British Judo Council when Kenshiro Abe
returned to Japan. Just five foot in height, he once wrote: 'Stomach throw,
major outer reaping, body drop, shoulder throw and propping ankle were
my favourite techniques, but groundwork was my best game'

12 There are few things more beautiful than a near-perfect throw, and the curious thing is that it almost doesn't matter whether you are the thrower or the thrown (see page 20)

13   By moving into a Moroto-Seoi-Otoshi half-pulling, half drawing yourself underneath your partner, Uke is totally controlled (see page 45)

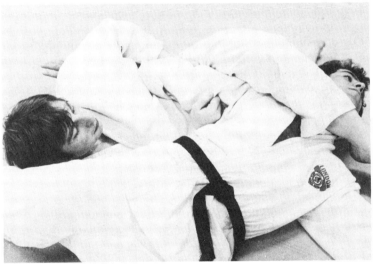

14a and b   It is crucial not to hang on grimly to a hold when your opponent
is escaping, but to have the presence of mind to use Uke's escaping
movement to change swiftly into something else. Here, Uke pushes out of the
Kesa-Gatame and Tori responds not by resisting but by twisting into a form
of Ude-Kujiki-Juji-Gatame (see page 56)

15a and b *(opposite)*   Being underneath one's opponent need not necessarily
be a hopeless place from which to counter-attack. Here Tori's position
(underneath) looks very weak, but, by making a small gap, he is able to use a

form of Hadaka-Jime. Tori's left hand slides over the back of Uke's neck, and grasps the sleeve of the right hand. The right hand moves to the right side of Uke's neck. It is not necessary for Tori's right hand to grasp his left sleeve, although this is also possible. In this photograph, the sleeve has slipped out of useful reach, but so long as Tori exaggerates the sliding action of his right hand, fingers outstretched, over the right side of Uke's neck, and so long as his left hand grip is very firm on his right sleeve, the technique can be very effective. We call this Sode-Jime, or sleeve choke (see page 56)

16 Kiri-Oroshi, the concluding technique of Kime-no-Kata. It is important to remember that Judo grew from the rich history of the Martial Arts of Japan and the techniques were and are of practical benefit. This kind of defence is appropriate whether the attacker holds a knife, a broken bottle or, as here, a Katana, a razor-sharp sword. Notice the controlled balanced posture which utterly dominates the failed lunge of the swordsman (see chapter 1 and page 72)

should be performed at a steady and methodical speed, to allow the differences in technique to be seen.

Ju-no-Kata

This Kata, the Kata of Suppleness, can be the most difficult of the Kata to perform if one is to avoid making it look mechanical. A point to note here, that should help in the understanding of the Kata, is that there is a constant change of negative-positive action between Uke and Tori, and Tori always finishes with a final positive technique. This Kata should be studied in three sets of five and practised in a smooth and steady continuous manner. It will be observed that this Kata shows the Ju-Jitsu origins of Judo, as the various attacking and defensive techniques demonstrate.

Kata of counters

There is no one Kata of counters practised as formally as the previous three. In the Kodokan, counters are taught by individual techniques, though elsewhere in Japan and Europe, Gonosen-no-Kata is broadening in popularity. A relatively recent addition to the Kata repertoire, Gonosen-no-Kata consists of twelve throws followed by twelve counters. More details are available from *The Complete 7 Katas of Judo* by M. Kawaishi, 7th Dan (Foulsham).

Kaeshi-no-Kata is an older form and demonstrates ten counters. In much the same way as in Gonosen-no-Kata, Uke attacks Tori slowly with a technique and throws. Tori then picks himself up and, when Uke attacks again, counters fast. This Kata can be divided into two sets of five. The late Yukio Tani passed this Kata on to Masutaro O-Tani who favoured this form rather than Gonosen-no-Kata, but the people able to demonstrate it are becoming few in number. Kaeshi-no-Kata shows the

71

control and precision that the good Judoka needs to improve his Judo and is a good basis for learning counter throws. Each of the techniques needs suppleness and movement from Tori and do not rely on strength.

Kime-no-Kata

This Kata – the Kata of Self-Defence Techniques – ably demonstrates the origins of Judo as a means of defence. It is also the first form which brings in striking techniques. Tori does not simply attack Uke without warning, but responds to Uke's attack. There are eight kneeling techniques (Idori) and twelve standing techniques (Tachi-ai). (The Japanese way of life was to kneel rather than to use chairs which is why the kneeling techniques are included.) A knife (Tanto) and sword (Katana) are used, but it is important to learn the correct use – the traditional weapons must be used in the proper form. This Kata helps to develop quick reactions to a variety of attacks, i.e. punching, cutting, kicking and holding, etc. There is also a different version of the Kata contained in Seiryoku-Zenyo Kokumin-Taiiku-no-Kata (the Kata of Physical Education-Maximum Efficiency).

Itsutsu-no-Kata

There are only five techniques in this Kata which symbolizes in a general way the forces of nature. This Kata was created by the late Dr Kano and he died before being able to name them so they are just numbered one to five. The first concerns one force overtaking and controlling another force travelling in the same direction, the second deflecting a force in another direction. The third is representative of a 'whirlpool' action, and the fourth is the action of the sea sweeping along the beach. The last of the set, number five, is of avoiding direct force by letting it expend itself. This is one Kata that needs a lot of practise to understand it fully. This form is the most difficult to perform with any meaning unless one dedicates much time and effort to Judo generally. Then and only then will Itsusu-no-Kata (The Forms of Five) make sense.

There are more Kata than just the seven mentioned here, such as Koshiki-no-Kata (Ancient Kata) and Goshin Jutsu-no-Kata but they are more rarely practised. They are, however, interesting and absorbing and would benefit Judoka of higher grades.

There is, of course, nothing to stop an instructor from compiling his own Kata, which could be a short self-defence routine for demonstrations or a mixture of throws and counters to enable the instructor to stress various aspects of Judo. Groundwork could also be included, and combination techniques for which no Kata is known to exist.

5 Home practice

There are very few people with such a natural affinity for Judo that they can afford to restrict practice merely to those occasions, once, twice or three times a week, when they come to a Dojo. A high degree of skill can only be developed when a daily practice and a fairly substantial daily practice at that, is maintained. Traditionally, in Japan, a Judoka who is serious about his Judo practises every day, even if he feels ill. If he has a bad muscle strain, he still comes on the mat, and does as much as he can. It is widely accepted that if a violinist or a pianist wants to develop a virtuoso technique, a practice of three, four or five hours is minimum. Yet there are very few Judoka in this country who practise with that level of diligence, and inevitably it means that the level of skill, particularly among the Dan Grades, is not high. There may not be many people able to regard Judo as a full-time activity, but it is possible to devote more time to one's practice, even when holding down an outside occupation, by working early in the morning at a Dojo, if that is possible, or at home.

There is a lot that can be done at home; in fact, there is a lot that should be done at home. The skilful Judoka has to learn to control himself before he can learn to control others. A substantial amount can be done alone, both in acquiring the basic movements of the whole range of standing and groundwork techniques, as well as, more obviously, developing fitness. Only when you can move with speed and precision, maintaining good posture throughout while you are on your own, are you really ready to work with a partner.

74

Fitness

Most of the exercises which are used in the Dojo can be repeated at home. The exercises should concentrate on stretching exercises to develop suppleness rather than weight-lifting or similar aids to develop strength. However, some ways of developing strength are useful: for instance, while there is little point (at least for the beginner) in doing press-ups, there is much value to be gained in doing pull-ups as the action helps to develop the pulling/turning action (Tsukuri) of the throw.

Work on stretching exercises more than strengthening. Flexibility in the hips is very important. This is an idealistic drawing of the foot to hand exercise – it is important to keep the legs straight and the twisting of the body down to a minimum, otherwise the hips will not benefit from the stretching action. If your foot is far from your hand at the beginning, don't contort your body to get nearer. Just practise with a straight leg daily. Do both sides

Tsugi-Ashi

Now let us study Tsugi-Ashi (footwork). If you place two slippers (Zoris) on the floor in the approximate position of your partner's feet and stand in front of them, you have acquired an invisible partner. Using the shoes as a guide, you can now

Back Bends 1 and 2. It is important to have a well-toned back, flexible and strong, in order to pre-empt injury. These are simple, but excellent exercises

practise different methods of turning in to your partner as in a throw, thus familiarizing yourself with the varying postures of different throws. When you next practise using a real partner, you will have already acquired some knowledge and will progress that much quicker.

The old maxim, 'Do not run before you can walk', is true

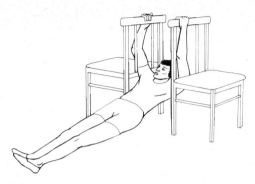

Where strength is needed in the thighs and the arms, particularly the forearms. Simple squats are very good for developing strength in the thighs; and pull-ups are very effective for developing the arms. Aim for 40–50 smooth pull-ups

when applied to Judo, but it does not mean that you must start at a crawl. Often students are taught the three-step movement at the beginning, but why, when two steps are quicker? Why take two steps when one will be even quicker?

This method of using Zoris as an invisible partner offers the Judoka the possibility of experimenting with different approaches to throws. Often, at the beginning, the Judoka is taught to turn in for Tai-O-Toshi, for instance, with three steps. But with his Zoris, he can practise turning in with just two steps, or even just one step. It also enables him to practise just as frequently with left-handed techniques. He can also learn to vary his approaches, sometimes using two steps, sometimes one and even, on occasions, three. Sometimes, when he turns in for a left-hand throw, he moves his left foot first. At other times, he moves his right foot first. If your Judo is based on a firmly founded and highly skilled footwork, then it will be fluid, fast and accurate. After all, Judo is a study of movement and if the movement of the feet is weak or limited, the whole of the movement will be weak.

Never accept second best. Kenshiro Abe used to say that only when one has performed a throw 100,000 times is one beginning

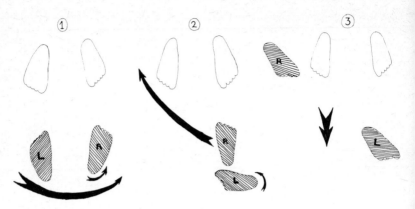

Practise at home with zoris acting as 'an invisible partner' as here – the Tai-Otoshi step-in

to understand that technique. This stepping in is crucially important and must be practised daily in order to improve one's speed, timing and knowledge.

Having established a firm foundation in Tsugi-Ashi, we can now start working on other aspects of throws. If you tie a push-bike inner tube to your belt and loop the belt around a hook or bannisters, or around the outside of a door handle (and then close the door on the belt) you find yourself once again with a 'partner'. A belt on its own is too inflexible to simulate a partner.

Taking the two ends of the belt, you can now improve your throwing movement by turning in on it, perhaps even placing a pair of Zoris on the floor to show your partner's feet position. Many throwing techniques such as Morote-Seoi-Nage or Harai-Goshi can be practised in this way. It is important to note that the belt does not slacken off as you turn in, as this means you are not sustaining the pull. Also, practise coming in to the Zoris from various positions and various distances. Make sure you are coming in as low as possible. For a technique such as Morote-Seoi-Nage, it is worth practising at times coming in and finishing deep on one's haunches, so that one can get in low,

Practise the complete turn-in, left and right, for the variety of Seoi-Nage and Koshi techniques with the help of a bicycle inner tube and then with an inner tube and zoris. Always maintain a critical frame of mind rather than slogging away to achieve a set work-rate. Look for sloppy aspects – bad posture, incorrect left-hand and right-hand action, imprecise foot movement, etc.

even with a partner in the defensive (Jigotai) posture. Always make sure that your own posture is strong and balanced at all points in the throw, but particularly at the beginning and the end.

Yoga

Up to now, we have concentrated on classic Judo exercises useful mainly for loosening up and strengthening specific areas of the body, and for building speed and precision in movement. Probably because the Western Judoka has had years of sitting in chairs and bending over desks, he is often very stiff in vital areas such as his hips and shoulders. Though it comes from a different culture, the ancient Indian discipline of Hatha Yoga has an enormous amount to offer the Judoka.

Hatha Yoga, which is well over 2,000 years old, is based on 'asana' or position. One of its foremost living practitioners is B. K. S. Iyengar of Pune, India, whose approach is reknowned for its rigour and precision of technique. It is this method of Hatha Yoga that is followed in this chapter.

Like some Western exercises, the asanas build and tone muscles and develop a sense of physical rhythm, but these are not their primary functions: more important are the release of locked energy and the development of a detailed empirical awareness of all parts of the body. This in turn leads to precise control over these same areas and allows the body to move in parts generally assumed to be immobile or inflexible. In this way, Yoga develops the physical suppleness for which it is justly famed. It opens up areas throughout the body because it emphasizes the *total* body, and muscular extension as much as contraction.

These are the general benefits, but there are more specific advantages for a Judoka in maintaining a basic but regular Yoga practice. All asanas can help him get further into throws by increasing flexibility in the hips, shoulders and armpits. Certain poses develop his sense of balance and rhythm, giving him more control in throws. Others may teach him to relax or breathe better, or may give him the flexibility to escape more easily from hold-downs and arm-locks. More detail is given in the description of each asana.

It must be stressed that, as in Judo, descriptions can be no substitute for classes with a competent Iyengar teacher. Such classes are taught in many towns in Britain and abroad.

Yogasanas (Yoga positions)

Yoga should be done on an empty stomach, two to three hours after any large meal; most people, however, do not find it uncomfortable to have a biscuit and tea half-an-hour before-hand.

The Standing Poses should be done on a clean, level floor that provides a good grip for the feet. These poses all strengthen the knees and protect them against damage – if one stands properly with straightened knees! In addition, they increase the flexibility of the hip-joints and shoulder girdle in different directions, increasing one's facility to get into throws and out of hold-downs. They all help the breathing by opening the chest. As well, they strengthen the ankles and legs, soothe backaches and increase flexibility in the neck, back, wrist and hands – which is obviously of benefit in both throws and groundwork.

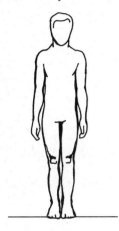

Tadasana (Mountain Pose)
Always start standing poses with this asana and come back to it between poses because this is the basic asana of good posture.

1 Stand with the toes and heels (or ankle bones) touching. The weight should be evenly distributed between heels and the metatarsal arches.
2 Straighten the knees completely by drawing the kneecaps back into the legs and upwards, using the quadraceps.
3 Tuck the tailbone down and forwards, and draw in the lower abdomen; lift up the length of the spine.
4 Open the top chest forwards and up; relax the shoulders and arms down and back without collapsing the spine.
5 Tuck the chin in slightly so that you are looking straight forwards (not up!).
6 Lengthen the entire back of the body upwards.

Trikonasana (Triangle Pose)
This pose strengthens and protects the knees. It aids the arm movements of throws by opening the upper chest, armpits and shoulders. As well, it increases the sideways flexibility of both hips and trunk.

1 Stand in Tadasana.
2 Inhaling, raise the hands to the chest; exhaling, jump the feet three to three and a half feet apart, simultaneously stretching the arms out at shoulder level, palms facing down. Arms should be parallel to the floor.
3 The feet should be parallel to each other, outside edges parallel, with the weight even on the inner and outer edges of both feet.
4 Stretch up with straight knees, tailbone tucked in slightly and top chest open. Throat and shoulders should be relaxed.
5 Turn the right foot out, ninety degrees to the right; turn the left foot in, slightly to the right. The heel of the right foot should be completely in line with the instep of the left foot. Keep both knees *completely straight* throughout the pose.

6 On an exhalation, stretch the trunk sideways to the right and hold the shin or the calf with the right hand.
7 Stretch the left arm straight up in line with the right arm. Lengthen the trunk. The legs, arms and trunk should be in the same plane. Tuck in the chin slightly and look up at the left hand with both eyes.
8 Breathing evenly, stay in the pose ten to twenty seconds.
9 Inhaling, come back up into position 4.
10 Now do the pose to the left by doing steps 5–8 to the left side.
11 Inhaling, come up; drop the arms and turn the feet to the front.
12 Exhaling, jump the feet together so that you are standing in Tadasana.

The two poses described below strengthen and protect the knees. They increase the ability to roll the thighs apart for greater control in groundwork and increase the general suppleness of the trunk. They also develop strength and control in dropping the body for throws such as Tai-Otoshi.

Virabhadrasana 2 (Second Warrior Pose)

1 Stand in Tadasana.
2 Inhaling, raise the hands to the chest; exhaling, jump the feet four to four and a half feet apart, simultaneously

stretching the arms out at shoulder level, palms facing down. Arms should be parallel to the floor.

3 The feet should be parallel to each other, with the weight even on the inner and outer edges of both feet.

4 Stretch up with straight knees, tailbone tucked in slightly, and top chest open. Throat and shoulders should be relaxed.

5 Turn the right foot out, ninety degrees to the right; turn the left foot in, slightly to the right. The heel of the right foot should be in line with the instep of the left foot. Keep the left knee completely straight!

6 Keep the trunk perfectly vertical; exhaling, bend the right knee so that the shin is vertical.

7 Check that the left hand has not dropped below shoulder level; turn the head and look along the right arm, keeping the head vertical. Stretch out the arms and hands power-fully. The back of the trunk, hips and legs should be in the same plane. Stay in the pose ten to twenty seconds.

8 Either (a) Straighten the right leg to come up and do the pose to the left by doing steps 5 to 7 to the left. Then go to step 12. Or (b) Continue into *Parsvakonasana* (Lateral Angle Pose). Exhaling, stretch the trunk to the right so that the right forearm rests on the knee. For greater stability, you can rest the right arm or hand on a low stool or platform.

9 Stretch out the left arm beyond the ear, in line with the
trunk and left leg. Tuck in the chin slightly and look up.
Keep the outer edge of the left foot pressing in to the
floor. Stay in this position ten to twenty seconds.
10 Inhaling, come back up into position 4.
11 Now do the pose to the left by doing steps 5–9 to the left.
12 Inhaling, come back up into position 4. Drop the arms and
turn the feet to the front.
13 Exhaling, jump the feet together so that you are standing in
Tadasana.

Uttanasana (Intense Stretch Pose)
(If you have low blood pressure, do this pose only under a
teacher's supervision.)

1 Stand in Tadasana.
2 Keep the head up and the chest open as long as possible:
exhaling, relax forwards from the hips and the bottom of
the spine, keeping the knees completely straight.
3 When you cannot bend down any further, relax the entire
upper body, but keep straightening the knees. Stay in the
pose ten to twenty seconds.
4 Inhaling, come up, raising the head and chest first.
5 Stand in Tadasana.

N.B. This is a fundamental relaxing asana which can be done at
any time during or outside a practice.

Home practice

Virabhadrasana I (First Warrior Pose)
This pose helps all the Goshi throws by increasing the rotational suppleness within the hips. As well, it improves arm movements by opening the upper chest and armpits.

1 Stand in Tadasana.
2 Inhaling, raise the hands to the chest; exhaling, jump the feet four to four and a half feet apart, simultaneously stretching out the arms at shoulder level.
3 Turn the palms upwards and stretch them over the head so that they touch. Tuck in the tailbone.
4 Exhaling, turn the right foot out ninety degrees to the right; turn the left foot well in, to the right. The hips and trunk should face to the right. The heel of the right foot should be in line with the instep of the left foot. *Keep the left knee completely straight.*
5 Exhaling, bend the right knee so that the shin is vertical. Keep on turning the left hip around to the right and stretching up the spine and trunk. Stay in the pose ten to twenty seconds.

6 Inhaling, straighten the right knee and return to position 4. Drop your arms and turn the feet to the front.
7 Recover the breath; inhaling, raise the arms to shoulder level; exhaling, stretch out through the hands.
8 Now do the pose to the left by doing steps 3–5 to the left.
9 Inhaling, straighten the left knee and return to position 4. Drop the arms and turn the feet to the front. Exhaling, jump the feet together so that you are back in Tadasana.

N.B. It is useful to work on this pose with hands on hips, concentrating on the lower body. This method is also useful if you are feeling tired, since this is an undemanding position.

Ardha Chandrasana (Triangle Balance Pose)
In the beginning it is very good to do this pose with the back against a wall. It helps Harai Goshi and O-Guruma by opening the hips laterally. It aids arm movements and breathing by opening the upper chest, armpits and shoulders. As well, balance is improved.

1 Same as Trikonasana 1–7.
2 Drop the upper arm along the trunk. Bend the right knee

87

and place the right fingers on the floor about twelve inches
beyond the right foot. Bring the left foot slightly closer to
the right.

3 Exhaling, swing the left leg up parallel to the ground and
  straighten the right leg completely.

4 Lift the left hip up and back so that it is vertically over the
  right hip. Stretch the left arm up, palm facing forwards,
  and roll the chest towards the ceiling. Tuck in the chin
  slightly and look up. Stay in the pose ten to twenty
  seconds.

5 Drop the upper arm, bend the right knee and place the left
  foot on the floor. Straighten the right knee and return to
  Trikonasana. Inhaling, stand up.

6 Now do the pose to the left by doing Trikonasana and then
  steps 2–4 to the left.

7 Come out of the pose via Trikonasana and return to
  Tadasana.

N.B. If your hips are not very flexible, it is useful to do this pose
resting the bottom hand on a brick or stool.

The sitting poses should be done on a floor covered by a carpet,
mat or firm blanket. We have selected these poses for their
powerful effect in opening up the hips, chest and shoulders.

Virsana (Hero's Pose)
This way of sitting increases flexibility in the knees, feet and ankles. The arm and hand action opens the shoulders for Goshi throws as well as curing hand and wrist stiffness, for better control in all throws.

1 Kneel with the legs together and the buttocks resting on the heels. Stretch the trunk straight up.
2 If you are comfortable, separate the feet so that the buttocks rest on the floor between the feet. The feet should point back, directly away from the knees.
3 Interlock the fingers and stretch the arms above the head, palms up. Stay in the pose thirty to sixty seconds.
4 Lower the hands, change the interlock of the fingers and repeat for the same length of time.
5 Release the hands and proceed to *Gomukhasana* (Cow-Face Pose). You can remain kneeling, sit cross-legged, stand or even sit on a chair so long as your back is erect.
6 Take the left hand up the back, drawing the elbow in with the right hand.

7 Stretch the right arm straight up. Then bend the elbow and drop the right hand down to the left hand. Clasp hands or wrists. Stay in the pose thirty to sixty seconds.
8 Now do the pose on the other side for the same time.

N.B. If your hands do not touch in Gomukhasana, do the pose with a belt in the upper hand. The lower hand can then grasp the belt as well and you can work your hands together.

Baddha Konasana (Cobbler's Pose)
By powerfully opening and turning the hips, this pose is excellent for groundwork, both for escaping and for controlling your opponent between your legs.

1 Sit on the floor with the legs stretched forwards together.
2 Bend the knees and draw the feet towards the groins. Clasp the soles together with the hands and draw the heels as close as possible to the perineum.
3 Stretch the back up vertically and let the knees sink towards the ground by relaxing the hips. Do this pose as often and as long as possible, being careful not to tense or raise the shoulders.

Upavistha Konasana (Seated Angle Pose)
The benefits of this pose are similar to those of Baddha Konasana.

1 Sit on the floor with the legs straight forwards.
2 Take the legs sideways as far apart as possible, keeping the knees completely straight and the feet vertical.

3 Place the fingers on the floor behind the buttocks and stretch up the trunk from the base of the spine without raising the shoulders. Stay in the pose ten to thirty seconds. Relax and try again.
4 Carefully release the knees.

Sarvangasana (Shoulder Stand)
It is especially important *not* to do this pose on a bare floor. Sarvangasana gives the suppleness of neck and upper back necessary for escape from hold-downs such as Kata-Gatame. It also improves breathing by opening the chest.

1 Lie flat on the back in a straight line, with the feet together and the hands beside the body.
2 Bend the knees over the trunk. Pressing the palms into the ground, exhale and swing the trunk vertically and support the back with the hands. Carefully straighten the legs so that the body is in a vertical plane.
3 The hands should support the back as close to the floor as possible so that the back is straight. Keep the knees straight and the feet together. Stretch up in this pose for a minute or more, gradually working up to five minutes with practice.
4 Exhaling, bend the knees and gently roll down.

91

Savasana (Corpse Pose)
This is an invaluable relaxation.

1 Lie flat on the back with sufficient *loose* clothes or covers to remain warm but not restricted. The feet should touch each other.
2 Use your hands to tuck the skin on the buttocks towards the feet. Stretch out each heel fully and release both legs completely.
3 The arms should lie just far enough apart to avoid contact with the body. Palms face upwards. Release the arms completely.
4 Lift the head and check that you are still in a straight line. As you place the head back on the ground, tuck in the chin slightly to lengthen the neck. Close the eyes and release the neck.
5 Take your awareness to the feet and from there gradually pass through the entire body, consciously relaxing each part of the body and withdrawing your awareness from it until you are only aware of the breath in the lungs. Keep the attention on the breath for the remainder of the pose.
6 Ideally, Savansana should be done for ten to fifteen minutes. If this is not possible, stay at least five minutes in the pose. Gradually, come out of the pose, opening the eyes and rolling over on to your side. Remain on each side for about ten to twenty seconds before getting up.

Practice

Work through all the poses we describe in order to discover which help you most in your own Judo: perhaps it is asanas that open the hips, perhaps ones that strengthen the knees. Then incorporate the appropriate poses into your daily Judo practice to help your body with its specific problems. If you discover – as is quite likely – that you need to work on knees, hips, upper back, chest . . . then vary your practice poses from day to day accordingly.

It is a good idea once a week to do a full practice of all the poses we describe. This will take about forty minutes.

Standing poses are often best practised in the morning, sitting poses in the evening, but they can be practised together at any time. Do Uttanasana after every other standing pose, or whenever necessary. And finish every practice with Savasana.

Regardless of the length of your practice, neither rush through it nor waste time between poses. Aim eventually to hold standing poses for about twenty seconds on each side and the other poses for longer periods.

Daily Judo and Yoga practice

It is a good idea to develop a daily practice which can be done every morning before breakfast or before supper or both. Each individual needs different practice, so it is best to set a routine for oneself, but what follows is a suggested routine which would benefit most Judoka. It lasts thirty minutes, or twenty-five minutes with a concluding Savasana relaxation.

Three Standing Yoga Asanas, two minutes each.
Three Sitting Yoga Asanas, two minutes each.
Situps, one minute.
Pull-ups, one minute.
Stepping Practice: 2 step practice (left and right), one
                   minute,
                   1 step practice (left and right), one
                   minute.
Tsukuri on the belt: fourteen minutes.

Divide the time equally between left and right, with various stepping and hand actions – O-Goshi, Harai-Goshi, Seoi-Otoshi, Tai-Otoshi, Sode-Tsuri-Komi-Goshi, etc. Perhaps pick three techniques to work on each week, left and right, varying the stepping/approach action. Beware of allowing repetition to breed sloppy habits – each turn-in must be approached with a fresh and critical mind.

Savasana: five minutes, if possible.

6 Meditation and Judo

An encounter with Judo is an encounter with an entire ethos in which one is constantly being urged to develop new qualities as a human being. One is encouraged to develop the confidence that arises out of fearlessness. One has to learn to accept discipline from the Sensei, from the subtleties of the art itself, and from oneself.

With progress, one finds that qualities of integrity and harmony are developed; there is no room in Judo for arrogance, selfishness and mental or physical clumsiness, and one should find that a fundamentally non-violent, compassionate outlook is being developed, largely because when we have less to fear, we are able to be more open to the needs of others and because when we are aware of our own limitations, then we are less likely to be carping and critical of others.

Judo demands constantly that we go beyond ourselves in our exertions on the mat, in our pursuit of excellence in technique. It is impossible to reach a point where one can relax with the satisfaction that the end has been reached: improvement is always possible.

The really important changes, however, are those which take place in the totality of one's being. It is often not long after starting Judo that people begin to realize that they are changing in a much broader way than one would expect by the acquisition of a fighting technique and an improved physical fitness. Such a vision of the Gentle Way is soundly reinforced by looking at the example of the masters of martial arts: it is worth noting that

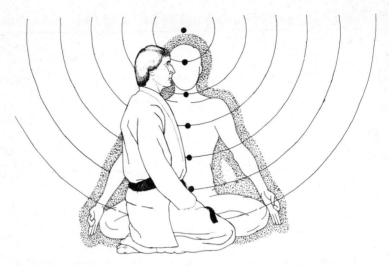

The real magic of Judo is the way it enables us to change and develop as people, on and off the mat. Judo trains the mind and the body, but it is of invaluable benefit to train the mind directly. Here, meditation is the tool. By the regular practice of meditation, we truly choose what we want to do – to act rather than react – as well as developing far greater control and awareness of our own bodies

most of the well-known Japanese figures (such as the swords-man Musashi) ultimately regarded meditation as the central quest, and the true culmination of so many years of effort in the Dojo. Why is this?

The importance placed upon change, on the development of qualities such as integrity, self-discipline and compassion, binds Judo to its Japanese roots far more deeply than all the Japanese names and words that are common currency in the Dojo, or the external formalities, such as bowing, that are observed there. Japan is a country where for hundreds of years the spiritual tradition of Buddhism has made its influence felt. These qualities, and the urge to change, are characteristic elements of the Buddhist approach to life.

Unlike most major religions, Buddhism is not based on the revelation of some divine teaching. It is a religion with no god.

Put very simply and briefly, the essence of Buddhism is a vision of what every human being could be. Buddhism suggests that each of us, were we to unfold our full potential, could be 'Buddhas', enlightened beings, supremely wise to the reality of things, suffused with unbounded love and compassion, and utterly free from all limitations of the purely conditioned mind.

For two and a half thousand years a whole universe of teachings and recommendations about the path to enlightenment has grown up around the original teachings of Gautama the Buddha, the founder of the tradition. The Buddha lived in northern India, but the Buddhist teachings spread widely thoughout Asia. Today Buddhist teachers and teaching centres are increasingly easy to find in the West.

Wherever they have travelled, people have looked for ways of adapting the Buddhist teachings to make them relevant to their own cultural backgrounds, temperaments and spiritual needs. An almost diagrammatic instance of this principle is provided by a look at the way the 'Buddha rupa', or statue of the Buddha has been used. An Indian rupa will show us an Indian Buddha, one from Tibet, a Tibetan, and one from Japan will portray a Japanese Buddha. To be a Buddhist does not mean that you conform to a set of dogmas external to yourself, but that you are doing your best to be what *you* really can be, and making use of the collected wisdom of the Buddhist tradition in doing so.

Perhaps it is because of a particularly practical streak in the Japanese temperament that the Japanese version of Buddhism has always had more to do with *doing* than with words. For example, the word *Zen* means meditation, and Zen Buddhism is a form of Buddhism in which the practice of meditation takes precedence over merely conceptual considerations.

The Japanese seem to have a genius for turning simple tasks such as tea-making, or flower-arranging into 'dos', ways of achieving self-mastery and perfection. In exactly the same way, martial arts such as swordsmanship and unarmed combat – which even as purely physical disciplines make huge demands on their practitioners – have been gently moulded into spiritual disciplines, into instruments of change.

Judo therefore has far more than a casual relationship with Buddhism and with meditation, the central 'tool' of Buddhist practice. In its purest form, Judo is a Buddhist practice, and has a blood kinship with meditation. In what that kinship consists we are now going to see.

Because in the West the word meditation is being used to cover a startling array of techniques – many of which have nothing to do with meditation at all – there is a tremendous amount of confusion as to what it is. Does it mean making your mind blank? Does it involve turning a lofty religious theme over and over in your mind? Is it an antidote to stress and overwork? Is it a path to psychedelic experience?

According to Buddhist tradition at least, meditation is the most direct method of working on the mind in order to raise your level of consciousness.

This short description requires a little amplification. What is meant by 'raising your level of consciousness'? And why is meditation the most direct method? These questions can best be answered by suggesting a way in which consciousness can be raised *indirectly*. And immediately we find ourself back with Judo, back in the Dojo.

You have no doubt had the experience of going along to a practice session feeling tired and listless after a hard day's work. Perhaps you would feel better about going straight home for a relaxing evening. But you go along just the same.

To begin with your efforts are a bit half-hearted, as you perform the loosening up exercises. But gradually, as you begin to make a bit of an effort, as you fill your lungs with deep breaths, as you are urged to push beyond your initial resistance to the demands of the exercises, you start to take a pleasure in the activity. Energy starts to pump back into you, the cobwebs fall away. You give more attention to the flow of your move-ments, concentrating to stay in balance, in tune with yourself and with your partners. Soon you are feeling completely different: not just physically and mentally alert and supple, not just in touch with your energy, but enriched and refined by the need for a pin-sharp awareness of everything that is taking place. You leave the Dojo at the end of the session walking on air, thoroughly at home in your skin, calm and centred, confident and alive. Your state of consciousness has been transformed almost beyond recognition – indirectly by your efforts on the mat. This is what can happen to you in just one evening. Regular practice takes the process further and deeper, extending the transformation to more and more aspects of our being.

Almost any form of physical exercise can have an enlivening effect on our state of consciousness, but no doubt the discipline, the atmosphere and the particular demands of the Dojo ensure that a technique like Judo will have a far more wide-reaching effect on us than will some other less precise, less harmonious activity.

By now it should have become clear what is meant by 'raising one's state of consciousness'. It involves becoming more aware, more alert, more awake. It means becoming more concentrated, more integrated, and also more emotionally rich, open and refined. In a word, it means becoming more truly, creatively *alive*.

There are, of course, many more ways in which we can work, indirectly, on our state of consciousness. Indeed, *everything* we do has some effect on our state of consciousness. But if we want to raise our level of consciousness we can take up an artistic pursuit, such as painting, modelling, or flower arrangement, or we can put ourselves with the 'aesthetic dimension' by attending concerts, plays and so on. We can spend time in the countryside, allowing the natural beauty to permeate and uplift us. We can enjoy deep, meaningful communication with our friends. We can experiment with a more harmonious, disciplined life-style which frees us from unnecessary strain, or neurotic over-stimulation. In Buddhist literature the mind is sometimes likened to a treasure-chest. There are innumerable ways in which we can delve into it and discover the gems that lie there –

just as there are innumerable ways in which we manage to lock ourselves out of it so much of the time!

By taking up, and seriously practising one or more of these indirect methods we can carry ourselves a very long way. One only has to meet a Judo instructor, or gifted musician, to notice very quickly that those people who devote themselves whole-heartedly to such pursuits are more alive, in a sense more human, than most other people we meet.

There is, however, even further to go. As human beings our capacity for growth and further development is limitless; the treasure chest is, according to Buddhism anyway, bottomless. Beyond our present level of existence stretch inconceivable peaks of awareness, emotional warmth and positivity, and freedom. To scale those higher peaks, however, we will need more than indirect methods. We will need a powerful direct method of working on ourselves. We will need meditation.

When we meditate, we no longer work on our state of consciousness by way of our senses or our bodies: we begin instead to work directly on our minds, with our minds. A meditation practice is a technique which allows us to do this. Perhaps I should give you an example of a meditation practice so that you can get an idea of how it all works.

The Mindfulness of Breathing is a very basic meditation technique. It is also extremely old. The Buddha himself taught it 2,500 years ago, and he did not invent it. So this practice can truly be said to have stood the test of time.

Briefly, the Mindfulness of Breathing is a concentration exercise. Nothing could be more basic than that. Unless you can concentrate, put your mind where you want to put it, in a calm, unforced way, you simply cannot undertake any other meditation practice. The same applies to Judo. Unless you can remain concentrated on what you are doing, but without being tensed up about it, you will be lost before you have even begun. To be able to concentrate you need something to concentrate on, and in this particular practice we use our own natural breathing process. Right from the outset I should make it clear that this is not a breath control exercise. It bears no relation to *Pranayama* which is practised by Yoga adepts. What we do is try to become more and more concentrated on our breathing, just as it is, just as it naturally comes.

Sitting comfortably, but with a straight back, our eyes closed or half-closed, with our hands resting on our laps, or loosely on our knees, we begin to focus our attention on our breathing. Our aim is gradually to allow all other thoughts and mental activities to give way to, become absorbed into our awareness of our breathing. This is not easy, and so the practice is broken up into four stages – which we practice for five to ten minutes each – which guide us naturally into ever deeper states of concentration.

In the first stage we watch our breathing, the in-flow and out-flow, and simply count, silently, one number at the end of each out breath. So we breath in, then out, and say 'One'; then in and out, and 'Two'. And so we continue, until we reach 'Ten'. We then start again at 'One'. Using the counting in this way we very quickly discover whether or not we are getting anywhere with the practice, for if our mind wanders even for a moment, we lose the count, and have to start all over again at 'One'.

The second stage is much like the first, only we count at the beginning of each inward breath. For some reason most people find this stage more difficult than the first. Perhaps because we have got the counting over with we feel free to go off and gather some wool for a moment. But the count gets lost, and we have to go back to the beginning again. In this way the second stage requires just a little more concentration from us, a little more commitment, than did the first.

In the third stage we drop the counting. Up until now that counting has acted as a kind of prop, pinning us to the practice, keeping us busy and interested. But now there is just the breathing, for five minutes, ten minutes, just the steady flow of our breathing, and we have to try to stay poised and concentrated on every breath. If we have made an effort in the first two stages we should find that this stage is not so difficult, for with

101

the concentration that we have built up comes a freedom from all the conflicting pulls that normally keep us in such a distracted state. We begin to enjoy the feeling of our breaths pouring in and out of us, rising and falling with the flow of it all, we become more and more wrapped up in it.

In the last stage we gather together our awareness, which has been until now spread over the entire breathing process, and focus it on that subtle sensation where the air first seems to make contact with out body as it enters us and where we feel it leaving us. There is no single fixed point. You may feel it in your nostrils, or on the top of your lip, or in the back of your throat. The point may even wander about; that does not matter. Simply allow your awareness to home in on the sensation, and focus more and more completely on it, until all your attention, all your awareness is truly 'one-pointed', truly concentrated. That is the basic practice.

When you take your place on a chair, or on a cushion in order to start this practice, it is more than likely that you will be quite unprepared for the shock that awaits you. Just as the newcomer to Judo thinks that the throws being demonstrated by the instructor look childishly simple – until he tries them for himself and discovers just how unsupple and uncontrollable his body is – the newcomer to meditation will be amazed to discover just how wild, slippery and untameable his mind is. Your own mind! You have been living with it for years; you think you know it; you think you have control over it. But can you stay concentrated on your breathing even for a couple of minutes without being overwhelmed by daydreams, anxieties and a whole army of other distractions? It really can seem hopeless.

With patience, practice, a lot of determination and energy, however, progress is made. Slowly but surely you manage to gather together the energies and elements of your everyday mind. You begin to focus and concentrate them, and for the first time in your life, perhaps, you experience yourself as a single, unified being with no mental chatter, no neurotic thought processes, no conflicts. You have arrived at the first stage of the meditation experience: the stage of concentration.

Perhaps this will be the first time that you have experienced this state of mind, but perhaps, after all, your practice of Judo, or another 'indirect' method, will have already given you some experience of it. The rapt musician or concert-goer, the inspired artist, the perfectly co-ordinated Judoka awaiting his partner's next move could all find themselves quite frequently touching on this beautifully clear, balanced state of consciousness. But there is far further to go.

When you listen to music, or perform a complicated move in Judo, there is always the outside element – the music itself, your partner, your physical sensations – that act as an anchor for your attention, to which you are bound. This relationship, though crucial to the effect of an indirect method, in a way determines the limits of the mental transformation that you can achieve. Your awareness of necessity stays rooted in the world of gross form. In meditation, however, one is not limited in this way. Herein lies the power of meditation practice.

Although you may become fully concentrated by watching your breath, once you reach the stage of concentration, an interesting phenomenon occurs. Gradually your experience of the breathing becomes more and more subtle and refined. It is as if the state of concentration itself takes over as the focal point of your awareness. You may even lose contact with your breathing altogether, though not in a careless forgetful way. After a while, even the experience of concentration becomes more subtle, until you are left poised in a state of radiant translucent awareness, seemingly surrounded by space and peace. You have entered what are known as the *Dhyanas*: the stage of meditative absorption. The word *Dhyana*, incidentally is the root of the Chinese word Cha'an, which is the root of the Japanese word 'Zen'.

These are very rich and powerful states indeed. Far from being unconscious and trance-like, they are intensely energetic, rich, inspired states of mind. You feel utterly calm, quite free of all gross limitations and concerns. You are completely in harmony with yourself, not just on the level of the conscious mind, but even on the deepest levels of the unconscious, saturated by all the wealth of those parts of your being from which you are normally barred.

Regular experience of these states not only gives you access to new layers of energy, new dimensions of inspiration, which will flow out into all the activities of your life, but it also serves as the necessary basis for the third and final stage of meditation, the stage of insight. The place and value of this aspect of meditation can be demonstrated by means of another analogue from Judo.

No matter how fit, bright and supple your practice of Judo makes you, you will lose most of the benefits it has to offer when you cease to practice regularly: some, but not necessarily all.

In the same way, no matter how high you reach in terms of meditative absorption, your feelings of bliss, clarity and energy will soon dissipate if you give up your regular practice; unless you have experienced insight.

When you take up Judo you soon realize that you have a lot of bad habits. The way you walk and stand is all wrong, conditioned by years of armchairs, or desk-work. As the teacher guides you through your preliminary exercises your mind keeps telling you that you have had enough when actually, your body is capable of doing a lot more. When someone makes a grab for you, you instinctively duck back, rather than going forward to meet him creatively. These are just some of the habits and conditioned attitudes that you bring with you into the Dojo, and you just have to realize that you have got things all wrong. Your normal ways are unhealthy, even unnatural. After a lot of concentrated practice you find not only that you are getting fitter and stronger, but that you are beginning to recognize, see through your bad habits, you are beginning to unlearn them and replace them with healthier more natural ways of moving and responding. If and when you stop practising Judo you will naturally lose a lot of your fitness and suppleness, but it is unlikely that you will ever fall back into those bad habits again, for you have grown beyond them; you have permanently changed.

Similarly, when we first come to meditation, we bring with us all kinds of bad habits of mind and attitude. We bring with us what is known in the Buddhist tradition as spiritual ignorance. We do not carry ourselves properly at all! We do not really understand ourselves, others, life, anything in fact. All our problems with life, all our frustrations and limitations stem from this ignorance.

The stage of insight then, is the stage of meditation in which we begin to see through our bad habits, undermine our ignorance, and catch glimpses of what is true, what is real. Certainly insight should not be considered as something dry and intellectual; it involves our entire being; it is a total process of seeing, of unlearning what is false and learning what is true.

Certainly experiences of insight are not restricted to people who meditate. Probably everyone has glimpses, from time to time, of how things are, beyond the veil of their mundane conditionings, experiences of a dimension that seems to transcend everything they have ever known, and yet which seems to be more valid than anything they have seen or felt before.

Meditation practice, however, is a very important way of ensuring that these experiences can be used, absorbed into the fabric of our lives. Just as it is of very little use for us to get some sudden insight into how we have to execute a particular Judo throw if our bodies doggedly refuse to comply with the way we would like them to flow, so there is little point in our having experiences of insight into ourselves, or into life itself, if our minds are too stiff and unyielding to make the changes that our insights seem to demand. Regular meditation practice, and particularly regular experience of the absorption states, provides us with foundations for our insight to rest on. It gives us the mental suppleness and pliability, the emotional positivity, the intensity of energy that we need to cut through our negative conditionings and to start growing in accordance with our highest vision.

Insight may come suddenly in a dramatic experience. Or, it may come slowly, gradually, imperceptibly: we simply realize that we are changing. For that is the hallmark of insight: that it changes us, permanently. We really see things more clearly; we are more alive, more real: there is no slipping back. This kind of change is the real purpose of meditation. Even within the Buddhist tradition there are thousands of different meditation techniques. Some help us to concentrate, others help us to work more directly on our emotions. Many of them are used as triggers for insight. But all of them have the ultimate purpose of helping us to change, to unfold our staggering potential as human beings.

Judo too is about change, about going beyond yourself as you are right now. If, when you make contact with a Dojo, you find that you are making contact with something more than a physical art, more than a foreign culture; if you find that you are making contact with something that is really universal: the urge to grow, to discover higher, truer states of being, then without doubt you will have made contact with at least something of the influence and timeless magic of meditation and Buddhism.

APPENDIX 1
Techniques in the Katas

A. Nage-no-Kata (forms of throwing)

Te-Waza (hand/arm techniques)
1 Uki-Otoshi   (floating drop)
2 Kata-Seoi   (shoulder throw)
3 Kata-Guruma   (shoulder wheel)

Koshi-Waza (hip techniques)
4 Uki-Goshi   (floating hip)
5 Harai-Goshi   (sweeping hip)
6 Tsurikomi-Goshi   (resisting hip)

Ashi-Waza (leg techniques)
7 Okuri-Ashi-Barai   (sweeping ankle)
8 Sasae-Tsurikomi-Ashi   (propping drawing ankle)
9 Uchi-Mata   (inner thigh)

Ma-Sutemi-Waza (techniques with back to floor)
10 Tomoe-Nage   (stomach or circle throw)
11 Ura-Nage   (rear throw)
12 Sumi-Gaeshi   (corner throw)

Yoko-Sutemi-Waza (techniques with side to floor)
13 Yoko-Gake   (side dash)
14 Yoko-Guruma   (side wheel)
15 Uki-Waza   (floating technique)

B. Katame-no-Kata (forms of groundwork)

Osae-Komi-Waza (holding techniques)
1 Kesa-Gatame   (scarf hold)
2 Kata-Gatame   (shoulder hold)

3 Kame-Shiho-Gatame	(upper four quarters hold)
4 Yoko-Shiho-Gatame	(side four quarters hold)
5 Kuzure-Kame-Shiho-Gatame	(broken upper four quarters hold)

Shime-Waza (strangle/choking techniques)

6 Kata-Juji-Jime	(half cross chokes)
7 Hadaka-Jime	(naked choke)
8 Okuri-Eri-Jime	(sliding collar choke)
9 Kata-Hajime	(single wing choke)
10 Yoko-Juji-Jime	(side cross choke)

Kansetsu-Waza (locking techniques)

11 Ude-Garame	(entangled armlock)
12 Ude-Hishigi-Juji-Gatame	(cross or step over armlock)
13 Ude Hishigi	(straight armlock)
14 Ude-Hishigi-Hiza-Gatame	(armlock with knee)
15 Ashi-Gatame	(leg lock)

C. Ju-no-Kata (forms of suppleness)

1	Tsuki-Dashi	(forward thrust)
2	Kata-Oshi	(shoulder push)
3	Ryote-Dori	(wrist hold)
4	Katamawashi	(shoulder turn)
5	Ago-Oshi	(chin thrust)

6	Kirri-Oroshi	(downward cut)
7	Ryo-Kata-Oshi	(double shoulder press)
8	Nanami-Uchi	(sliding cut)
9	Katate-Dori	(single wrist hold)
10	Katate-Age	(single hand raising)

11	Obi-Tori	(belt hold)
12	Mune-Oshi	(chest push)
13	Tsuki-Age	(upper cut)
14	Uchi-Oroshi	(downward blow)
15	Ryogan Tsuki	(eye thrust)

D.i. Kaeshi-no-Kata (forms of counter throwing)

1	De-Ashi-Barai to De-Ashi-Barai	(sweeping ankle into sweeping ankle)
2	O-Uchi-Gari to Ushiro-Goshi	(major inner reap into rear hip)

3 Ko-Uchi-Gari to Okuri-Ashi-Barai   (minor inner reap into double sweeping ankle)

4 O-Soto-Gari to Harai-Goshi   (major outer reap into sweeping hip)

5 Ko-Soto-Gari to Tai-Otoshi   (minor outer reap into body drop)

6 Hane-Goshi to De-Ashi-Barai   (spring hip into sweeping ankle)
7 Harai-Goshi to Ushiro-Goshi   (sweeping hip into rear hip)
8 Uchi-Mata to Te-Waza   (inner thigh into hand technique)
9 Koshi-Guruma to Utsuri-Goshi   (hip wheel into changing hip)
10 Ippon-Seoi-Nage to Uki-Waza   (single arm shoulder into floating technique)

D.ii. Gonosen-no-Kata (forms of countering)

1 O-Soto-Gari to O-Soto-Gari   (major outer reap to major outer reap)

2 Hiza-Guruma to Hiza-Guruma   (knee-wheel to knee wheel)

3 O-Uchi-Gari to De-Ashi-Barai   (major inner reap to sweeping ankle)

4 De-Ashi-Barai to De-Ashi-Barai   (sweeping ankle to sweeping ankle)

5 Ko-Soto-Gake to Tai-Otoshi   (minor outer dash to body drop)

6 Ko-Uchi-Gari to Sasae-Tsurikomi-Ashi   (minor inner reap to propping drawing ankle)

7 Kubi-Nage to Ushiro-Goshi   (neck throw to rear hip)
8 Koshi-Guruma to Uki-Goshi   (hip wheel to floating hip)

9 Hane-Goshi to Sasae-Tsurikomi-Ashi   (spring hip to propping drawing ankle)

10 Harai-Goshi to Utsuri-Goshi   (sweeping hip to changing hip)

11 Uchi-Mata to Sukui-Nage   (inner thigh to scooping throw)

12 Kata-Seoi to Sumi-Gaeshi   (single arm to corner throw)

Note: Whilst Gonosen is widely used, Kaeshi-no-Kata was used by the late Yukio Tani and his former student the late Masutaro Otani. Kaeshi is more favoured by the Editors.

E. Kime-no-Kata (forms of self-defence)

Idori (kneeling)

1	Ryote-Dori	(wrist hold)
2	Tsuki-Kake	(punch to stomach)
3	Suri-Age	(push to head)
4	Yoko-Uchi	(side fist blow)
5	Ushiro-Dori	(rear hold)
6	Tsuki-Komi	(thrust with knife)
7	Kirri-Komi	(downward cut)
8	Yoko-Tsuki-Komi	(side knife thrust)

Tachi-Ai (standing)

9	Ryote-Dori	(wrist hold)
10	Sode-Dori	(sleeve hold)
11	Tsuki-Kake	(punch to head)
12	Tsuki-Age	(upper cut)
13	Suri-Age	(push to head)
14	Yoko-Uchi	(side fist blow)
15	Ke-Age	(kick to testicles)
16	Ushiro-Dori	(rear hold)
17	Tsuki-Komi	(thrust with knife)
18	Kirri-Komi	(downward cut)
19	Nuke-Kake	(sword unsheathing)
20	Kirri-Oroshi	(downward sword cut)

F. Itsutsu-no-Kata

1	Ich	(one)	(direct concentrated energy – direct push)
2	Ni	(two)	(deflection – avoid and use Uki-Otoshi)
3	San	(three)	(circular energy or whirlpool – using form of Yoko-Wakare)
4	Shi	(four)	(action and reaction – as the sea sweeps clean the shore)
5	Go	(five)	(the void – using form of Yoko-Wakare)

Note: This Kata was devised by Dr Kano and names were never given to the techniques, so the authors have simply numbered the moves. In the second set of brackets are my own interpretations of the techniques and not necessarily the commonly known description. [A.F.]

APPENDIX 2
Japanese terms

Compiled by Kenshiro Abe, 8th Dan

Ago-oshi	Pushing; chin
Aiki-do	Way of harmony. Spirit
Aite	Opponent or contestant
Ashi-barai	Sweeping ankle
Ashi-garami	Entwining or entangling of leg
Ashi-no-ko	Instep
Ashi-no-ura	Sole
Ashiwaza	Ashi – foot or leg. Waza – techniques
Ashi-yube	Toe or toes
Atama	Head
Atemi	Hitting or attacking vital points
Awase-te-ippon	Point. Referee's word if contestant scores two half points
Awase-waza	Two hold points
Banbutsu Ruten	All things in the Universe are in a constant motion
Budo	Martial Way
Bujutsu	Martial Arts
Bushido	The Way of the Warrior
Butsukari	Special form of Randori in which one performs the attacking actions. Usually a student with teacher
Cho-wa Chowasure	Harmonious mental and physical reaction during practice
Chu-ii	Referee Terminology. Penalty
Chu-kan-setsu	Elbow lock
Daki-age	Point by raising opponent shoulder high from ground
Daki-wakare	Daki – to scoop up. Wakare – throw to the side
Dan	Step. Black-belt grade
De-ashi-barai	Advancing foot sweep
Do	Side of body
Do	Way or Path
Dojo	Judo exercise hall

Appendix 2 Japanese terms

Eri	Collar: lapel
Eri-jime	Strangulation by use of collar
Fusegi	Defence
Fushensho	Retirement during Tournament of contestant, thus leaving his opponent the winner
Go-shin	Body-defence (self-defence)
Go-shin Jutsu	Self-defence
Gyaku	Any locking action, reverse; counter
Gyaku-gesa	Reverse scarf-hold
Gya-ku-juji-jime	Reverse cross strangle
Hadaka	Naked
Hadaka-jime	Naked – strangle (without collar or lapel)
Hajime	Referee terminology. Begin
Hana	Nose
Hane	Spring
Hane-Goshi	Spring-hip throw
Hanshi	Highest grade in Judo
Hansoku	Breaking contest rules, attempting forbidden action
Hansoku-gachi	Decision to Hansoku
Hansoku-make	Loss of contest through Hansoku
Hantei	Referee term. The winner
Hara	Stomach
Harai	Sweeping
Harai-goshi	Sweeping loin throw
Harai-tsure-komi ashi	Sweeping drawing ankle
Hidari	Left
Hiki	Pulling
Hiki-komi (gaeshi)	Pulling into groundwork before attempting throw
Hiki-komi-gaeshi	Throwing or turning over opponent preparatory to groundwork
Hiki-wake	A draw in contest
Hitai	Forehead
Hiza	Knee
Hiza-guruma	Knee-wheel
Iai-do	Sword Way
Iai-jutsu	Sword Fighting
I-kai-sen	First contest in tournament
(ni-kai-sen)	Second contest
Ippon	Full point
Is-shin	Complete commital to an action
Ita-me-wake	Draw owing to injury
Itsu-tsu-no-kata	Five techniques symbolising nature
Iwanami	Last technique in Koshiki-no-kata
Ji	Inherited knowledge

112

Jigotai	Defence posture
Jogai	Outside mat area
Jonai	Inside mat area
Ju	Gentle
Judo	Gentle way
Judogi	Traditional costume worn by Judoka
Judoka	Person practising Judo
Judo-no-Seishin	Judo spirit
Juji-jime	Normal cross strangle
Ju-jitsu	System of self-defence before Judo
Jun-kesho	Semi-final
Juno-kata	Slow motion formal technique
Kaeshi	Counter
Kaeshi-waza	Technique of counter throw
Kake	Throwing act
Kami-shiho gatame	Upper four-quarters hold-down
Kanibasami	'Scissors' throw
Kan-setsu-waza	Lock technique
Kappo	Resuscitation technique
Karate	An art of self-defence without weapons, chopping, punching, kicking
Kata	Pre-arranged form
Kata-gatame	Shoulder holding
Kata-guruma	Shoulder wheel
Kata-ha jime	Single wing choke-lock
Kata-juji-jime	Half-cross strangle
Katamawashi	4th technique in ju-no-kata
Katame waza	Groundwork technique
Katate-age	10th technique in Ju-no-kata
Katatedori	9th technique in Ju-no-kata
Keage	15th technique in Kime-no-kata
Keiko	Judo practice
Kesa-gatame	Scarf-hold
Ki	Spiritual energy
Kiken-gachi	Win due to withdrawing opponent
Kirikomi	7th technique in Kime-no-kata
Kirioroshi	8th technique in Ju-no-kata, also 20th in Kime-no-kata
Ko daore	7th technique in Koshiki-no-kata
Kodokan	Hall for studying the Way
Kohaku-giai	Red and white two-team contest where winner remains on mat until beaten
Koka	Score – quarter point
Koshi	Hip
Koshi-guruma	Hip wheel
Koshiki-no-kata	21 Jujitsu techniques in formal style from Kito-ryu

Koshi-nage	Loin throw
Koshi-waza	Hip technique
Ko-soto-gake	Minor outside dash
Ko-soto-gari	Minor outside reap
Kouchigari	Minor inner reap
Kuatsu	Resuscitation technique
Kube	Neck
Kube-nage	Neck throw
Kumi-kato	Method of holding jacket
Kumu	Take hold of each other
Kuruma-daoshi	10th technique (koshiki-no-kata)
Kuzure-kami-shiho gatame	Broken upper four quarters
Kuzushi	Breaking of the opponent's balance
Kuzushi-kata	Method of posture disturbing
Kyoshi	Teacher grade
Kyu	To seek or to study
Kyu-do	Archery Way
Kyu-jutsu	Archery
Kyu Shin	Ball, perfect sphere
Maki-komi	Winding technique
Ma-sutumi-waza	Back or rear sacrifice technique
Mata	Thigh (inside area)
Me	Eye
Migi	Right
Miku-daki	No. 1 – Koshiki-no-kata
Mi-mi	Ear
Mizu-guruma	No. 4 technique from Koshiki-no-kata
Mizu-iri	No. 3 from Ura (Koshiki-no-kata)
Mizu-nagare	No. 5 – Koshiki-no-kata
Mokusu	Meditation
Momo	Thigh
Morote-gari	Two-handed throw by clasping opponent's legs
Mune	Chest
Muneoshi	No. 2 Juno-kata
Nage	Throw
Nage no kata	15 formal throws
Nage waza	Throwing technique
Name Juju jime	Normal cross strangle
Naname-uchi	No. 8 from Ju-no-kata
Ne-waza	Ground work
Ni-gi-ri-kata	Method of hand hold
Nu-kake	No. 19 Kime-no-kata
Nuki-shiai	Team contest in which winner stays on mat until beaten
Obi	Belt

Obi-otoshi	Belt drop
Obi-tori	No. 11 (Junokata) to hold belt
O-goshi	Major hip technique
O-guruma	Great wheel
O-kuri-ashi barai	Sweeping ankle throw
Okuri-eri-jime	Sliding collar strangle
Omote	Front
Omote-no-kata	First 14 techniques of Koshiki-no-kata
O-sae-komi	Referee word – holding
O-sae-komi-waza	Technique of holding
Oshi	Pushing
O-soto-gari	Major outer reaping
O-soto-otoshi	Major outer drop
O-uchi-gari	Major inner reaping
O-uchi-mata	Major or great inner thigh
Randori	General or free practice
Rei	Salutation or bow
Reigi	Method of salutation
Ren-raku-waza	Sequence technique
Renshi	High grade teacher
Renshu	Free practice or exercise
Ri	Personal understanding of Ji
Ritsu	This motion is rhythmic and flowing
Ryo-gan-tsuki	No. 15 in Ju-no-kata
Ryo-kata-oshi	No. 7 in Ju-no-kata
Ryoku-heki	No. 3 technique in Koshiki-no-kata
Ryote-dori	No. 1 Kime-no-kata also No. 3 Ju-no-kata
Ryu	Method or style
Ryu-setsu	No. 4 in Ura (Koshiki-no-kata)
Saka-otoshi	No. 5 Ura Koshiki-no-kata
Samurai	Japanese knight or warrior
Sasae-tsuri-komi ashi	Propping, drawing ankle
Sensei	Teacher or instructor
Sen-shu-ken	Champion title
Sen-shu-ken-tai kai	Championship
Seigo-ryu	Method of Jujitsu
Seoi	Shoulder
Seoi-nage	Shoulder throw
Seoi-otoshi	Shoulder drop
Shiai	Contest or game
Shiai-jo	Contest area
Shido	Warning
Shi-jen-tai	Natural posture
Shikoro-dori	No. 11 Koshiki-no-kata
Shikoro-gaeshi	No. 12 Koshiki-no-kata

Shime-waza	Technique(s) of strangling and choking
Shin	Universal truth
Shinai	Bamboo Practice Sword
Shin-ban	To referee
Shin-ban-ho	Method of refereeing
Shin-ban-in	The referee
Shi-sei	Posture
Shizentai	Normal posture
Sho Shin	Beginner's mind
So-atai-shiai	League contest
Sode	Sleeve
Sode-dori	No. 10 Kime-no-kata
Sode-tsuri-komi goshi	Sleeve resisting hip throw
Sore-made	Referees word: finish contest
Soto-gake	Outer dash
Soto-maki-komi	Outer winding
Sukui	Scooping
Sumi-gaeshi	Corner turn
Sumi-otoshi	Corner drop (hand technique)
Suriage	No. 13 of Kime-no-kata
Sutemi	Sacrifice
Sutemi-waza	Sacrifice technique
Suwaru	To sit down (Japanese style)
Suwara-seru	Referee terminology – to contestant who attempts forbidden action: Sit down
Tai	Body – No. 1 Koshiki-no-kata
Tai-otoshi	Body drop
Taki-otoshi	No. 14 – Koshiki-no-kata
Tani-otoshi	Valley drop. No. 9 Koshiki-no-kata
Tatami	Judo mat
Tate-shiho gatame	Overholding
Tatsute	Referee's word: standing
Tawara-gaeshi	Rice-bale throw
Ten-tori-Jiai	Two team contest each pair participating
Te-waza	Hand technique
Tomoe-nage	Stomach throw
Tori	Thrower in kata
Tsubami-gaeshi	Special style of walk, formal walk in kata; footwork
Tsukake	No. 11 Kime-no-kata
Tsuki-age	No. 13 Juno-kata, also No. 12 Kime-no-kata
Tsuki-dashi	No. 1 Juno-kata
Tsu-komi	No. 6 Kime-no-kata
Tsu-komi-jime	Thrusting chokehold
Tsukuri	Breaking of posture prior to actual throw
Tsurikomiashi	Drawing ankle

116

Tsurikomigoshi	Resisting hip throw
Uchi-komi	Practice of technique without throw; repetition
Uchi-kudaki	No. 8 Koshiki-no-kata
Uchi-maki-komi	Inner winding
Uchi mata	Inner thigh
Uchi-oroshi	No. 14 Ju-no-kata
Ude	Arm
Ude-garami	Arm entanglement
Ude-kujiki-hiza gatame	Knee arm lock
Ude-kujiki-juji gatame	Cross arm lock
Ude-kujiki-ude gatame	Arm crush
Uke	Receiver in kata
Ukemi	Art of falling
Uki-goshi	Floating hip
Uki-otoshi	Floating drop
Uki-waza	Floating throw
Ura	Rear (formal word)
Ura-nage	Rear throw
Ura-no-kata	Second part of Koshiki-no-kata
Utsuri-goshi	Changing hip
Waki	Armpit
Waki-shita	Under armpit
Wan-kan-setsu	Arm lock
Waza	Technique
Waza ari	Three-quarter point
Yama arashi	Storm on the mountain
Yamete	Referee word: Stop (contest)
Yoko	Side
Yoko gake	Side dash
Yoko-guruma	Side wheel
Yoko-otoshi	Side drop
Yokoshiho-gatame	Side four quarters
Yoko-sutemi waza	Side sacrifice throw
Yoko uchi	No. 4 and 14 Kime no kata
Yoko-zuki	No. 8 Kime no kata
Yubi	Finger
Yudachi	No. 13 Koshiki-no-kata
Yuko	Half point (score)
Yusei	Referee word: decision
Yume no uchi	No. 2 Koshiki-no-kata
Yusei gachi	Referee word: decision on superiority
Yusho sen	Final (contest)
Zen	Silent meditation
Zori	Sandals